Praise for *God Made That!*

"'We have received a garden from the Creator, we must not leave a desert to our children,' Pope Francis repeats often. I believe *God Made That!* effectively responds to this appeal, solidly inspired by Catholic tradition, ranging from Saint Francis of Assisi to Saint Kateri Tekakwitha."

—Fr. Joshtrom Isaac Kureethadam, Vatican Dicastery for Promoting Integral Human Development

"This detailed handbook will not only help children to better observe the world around them but will also open up their eyes to see the beautiful interconnectedness of God's creation. Combining instruction on ecology, saint stories, prayer and Scripture readings, an intro to Catholic Social Teaching, and tons of practical, child-centered activities, this book is sure to be a fun and educational addition to any Catholic kid's library, teaching them that faith and science indeed go hand in hand!"

—Katherine Bogner, teacher, author, and blogger at LookToHimAndBeRadiant.com

"I enthusiastically recommend *God Made That!* for anyone with school-age children in their life. Its friendly and approachable text provides an abundance of spiritual and scientific information. As a result, it leads to a better understanding of God's creation as both a gift and a responsibility. . . . As the mother of two children in elementary school, I was pleased to see that the book has information, activities, and spiritual examples for environments ranging across forests, lakes, deserts, seashores, and even tundra, so that no matter where you live—or where your family may travel on vacation or pilgrimage—you can use this field guide to develop a deeper appreciation for nature and its Creator. *God Made That!* is a kid-friendly education in both theology and ecology. I recommend this guide for anyone who wants children to develop a sense of gratitude for and responsibility toward God's gift of our common home."

—Melissa Miscevic Bramble, Director of Operations,
Saint Kateri Tekakwitha National Shrine

"*God Made That!* is a beautiful and wholesome educational resource that wonderfully combines faith and science. The combination of saints, nature, activities, and learning makes this book a must-have for all families desiring an interactive faith-based education for their children."

—Kelsey Westman, homeschooling mom and content creator
at Faithful Acres Farmhouse

"This is exactly the kind of book I would have obsessed over as a kid. It's bursting at the seams with wonder and adventure! Beautifully grounded in Sacred Scripture and Tradition, *God Made That!* breaks open the gift of creation in a way that fosters vibrant stewardship, true brotherhood, and a lived relationship with God. Weaving together the truths of our faith, the wonders of scientific discovery, and the wisdom of traditional land knowledge, *God Made That!* offers a treasure for the classroom, the home, and the field! Whether poring over its fascinating facts indoors on a rainy day or carting it along as a guide on an outdoor adventure, children are sure to find inspiration for their walk with God here on Earth."

—Sr. Orianne Pietra René Dyck, FSP,
author of *Dive Deep: 40 Days with God at Sea*

"As an Indigenous Catholic catechist of the Akwesasne Mohawk Nation Turtle Clan, I highly endorse the book *God Made That!* For me, this text represents the sacred circle of life. Its holistic approach reminds us that God is the center and source of all creation. Therefore, the challenge for us is to live in harmony with God, the environment, all peoples, and the biodiversity of the many species on mother Earth, our common home. By reflecting with Scripture, Catholic Social Teaching, and our own personal stories, we become more aware of our relationship and interconnectedness to all of God's creation. We are all relatives. This excellent resource is educational and leads one to reflection, prayer, and action. It is a wonderful tool for educators, parents, and learners of all ages."

—Sr. Kateri Mitchell, SSA

"'Be praised, my Lord, for . . .' Saint Francis of Assisi celebrated and praised the fact that everything in God's creation is connected. He called the sun his brother and the moon his sister. *God Made That!* is a testament to the spirit of Saint Francis and Saint Kateri. Readers, young and old, will enjoy this excellent book and be filled with the Spirit as they turn each page."

—Friar Michael Heine, OFM Conv., Minister Provincial, Our Lady of the Angels Province

"*God Made That!* is a must-have resource for anyone seeking to protect, cherish, and embrace Earth, our common home. Packed full of beautiful art, factual data, activity ideas, and companionship of the saints, this field guide will be a living, breathing gift for any family or classroom. I can't wait to venture out and explore with *God Made That!*"

—Lisa M. Hendey, author of *I Am Earth's Keeper*

"Caring for God's incredible creation is so deeply embedded within our Scriptures and the deep history of our faith and written into our very biological processes. *God Made That!* does an amazing job of connecting our Earth to our faith, Scriptures, saints, and our God, and will inspire a deep sense of awe and wonder in every reader through a better understanding of our home from the broad sense down to the plants and birds. Reading this book gave me great joy and a rooted sense of connection to our Creator!"

—Anna Johnson, Senior Programs Manager, *Laudato Si* Movement

GOD MADE THAT!

CATHOLIC NATURE FIELD GUIDE

BY KATHLEEN M. HOENKE AND WILLIAM A. JACOBS

ILLUSTRATED BY FIONA OSBALDSTONE

Pauline
BOOKS & MEDIA
BOSTON

Nihil Obstat: Reverend Joseph Briody, S.S.L., S.T.D.

Imprimatur: ✠ Seán P. Cardinal O'Malley, O.F.M. Cap.
Archbishop of Boston
May 10, 2023

Library of Congress Control Number: 2023935900

ISBN 10: 0-8198-3164-6
ISBN 13: 978-0-8198-3164-4

Illustrated by Fiona Osbaldstone

Design by the Daughters of St. Paul

Published by Pauline Books & Media, 50 Saint Paul's Avenue, Boston, MA 02130-3491

Printed in the U.S.A.

www.pauline.org

Pauline Books & Media is the publishing house of the Daughters of St. Paul, an international congregation of women religious serving the Church with the communications media.

1 2 3 4 5 6 7 8 9 30 29 28 27 26 25

For Finn and Ella, may you forever wander in the wonders of nature,
finding in its beauty a path that leads you to God.

—K.H.

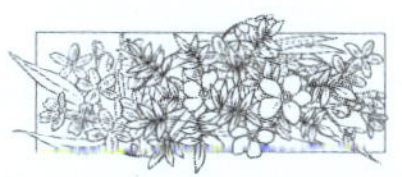

To my parents, Julia and Walter, and my grandparents, for their faith, love, and respect for people and nature. To my beloved wife, Lynn, my wonderful children, Erin, Cara, and Willy, and their spouses, and my precious grandchildren, Jacob and Jonah, who bring joy to my life.
A special dedication to Cristina Gaztelu Vargas,
whose faith and courage have been invaluable.

—B.J.

CONTENTS

PART 2

FOREWORD

The brilliant and faith-filled authors of this field guide have spent many years observing God's beautiful design in nature. They have studied the important role humans have in protecting it.

Exploring our world helps us grow in love and understanding of God and his awesome creation. Bill Jacobs, one of the authors of this book, once said to me that so much of the trouble in the world is because we "have lost our relationship with the land. We have forgotten where we've come from." He's right. God speaks to us through nature, which is why it can be so much easier to slow down, think, and pray outdoors.

My favorite feature of *God Made That!* is the traditional wisdom of Indigenous peoples that is skillfully woven in with scientific information and prayerful thanksgiving. We can learn so much about how to care for nature from the original people of this continent. Who better to learn from than those who have thrived on North American land for tens of thousands of years?

I am an enrolled citizen of the Mohawk Nation. This means that my ancestors were the original inhabitants of eastern New York State. I am from the same tribe as Saint Kateri Tekakwitha, a holy Mohawk woman who loved God and nature. Mohawks and other Indigenous communities believe that, when making decisions, it is important to think of the people who haven't been born yet. This is known as the Seventh-Generation principle. This is especially important when interacting with the environment. God calls us to take care of the Earth so that it will be just as beautiful and abundant for our grandchildren and their grandchildren.

I am so excited for you to experience this field guide. It is full of mind-boggling facts, captivating stories, and delightful activities for exploring where you live. It will help you learn and appreciate how people live in communion with nature, and what we can do to help care for this gift from God. God gave us this very important job from the beginning of creation. As an Indigenous person, I am thrilled to know that young Catholics are learning about nature in a way that honors traditional wisdom and love of our Creator. I hope you love it as much as I do.

Shauna'h Fuegen, OFS

PREFACE

Welcome to this field guide!

This is a guide to our homes on Earth, the places where human beings live, including habitats, ecosystems, and biomes, and the characteristic species of plants (***flora***) and animals (***fauna***) that live on the Earth. It is also a guide to how our experience of ***nature*** can help us connect with God and grow in our friendship with him. God created the world as a gift to us and wants us to enjoy exploring it!

This field guide is inspired by Catholic ecology. ***Ecology*** is the study of the relationships between people, plants, animals, and all other living things and their physical surroundings. These physical surroundings are also called the ***environment***, which is made of both living and non-living things. Plants, animals, and non-living things are created by God. They are by *nature* destined for the ***common good*** of past, present, and future humanity. People are called to be good stewards of ***creation*** (all that God has created), beginning with the places where we live.

This book talks about the science of ecology. It also looks at what the Bible and the Church teach us about our relationship with the world and each other. As we explore creation and see how it helps us become closer to God, we are following in a long line of people who have done the same thing. Throughout this book we will meet saints and other members of the Church who give an example of loving and caring for all God's creatures.

Some of the words that might be new for you are defined in the glossary beginning on page 187. The first time they are used they are in bold italics—***like this***.

This guide can be used anywhere—at home, in the classroom, or in the field. It offers a way for us to learn on our own, and it can also help parents and teachers teach ecology as an integral part of our Catholic faith. Some activities are best used in the biome of that chapter, and some can be done anywhere. Most of the activities are meant to get us outside, observing and exploring nature!

PREPARE TO EXPLORE!

Nature Safety

- Go with a friend, family member, or teacher. Use the buddy system.
- Always ask permission and let someone know where you will be and when you are coming back.
- Learn about an area before you go. If you are exploring a park, is there a map? Are there any hazards such as wide streams or steep hills that might pose a problem? Are the trails marked? Is the nature hike too long?
- Check the weather before you go.
- Drink water before, during, and after outdoor activities.
- Bring whatever you may need in the field, such as water, snacks, warm clothes, sturdy shoes, compass, whistle, insect repellent, cell phone, sunscreen, and a hat.
- Look down for holes, rocks, logs, mud, sharp sticks, steep cliffs, and anything else you might step on, trip over, fall into, slip on, or get stuck in.
- Look up for standing dead trees (called *snags*), sharp branches, broken tree limbs, wires, and anything else that might fall or be dangerous. Do not touch wires.

- Do not swim or go into water alone.
- Remember road safety. Watch out for cars when you're near a road.
- Learn to identify and avoid poison ivy and other poisonous plants and berries. Poison ivy has groups of three leaves, and we say, "Leaves of three, let it be." Not only should you not eat any plant that has not been positively identified, but you should also wash your hands before eating or even before touching your face, in case you have come into contact with something poisonous.
- Watch out and listen for snakes, wasp nests, bears, mosquitoes, and other potentially dangerous wildlife.
- Avoid getting stung by a bee, wasp, yellow jacket, hornet, or fire ant. Some people may have a serious allergic reaction to insect stings.
- If you live in an area with ticks, try to avoid tall grass and brush. Use a tick repellant if needed, with adult supervision. Check your clothes as you go and check yourself carefully for ticks when you get home. Remove ticks promptly, within twenty-four hours.
- Be careful about too much heat. (Young children can overheat quickly and at lower temperatures than adults.) Take frequent breaks in the shade and drink plenty of water.
- Know who to call and where to go in an emergency.
- If you get lost, stay put in a safe place until help arrives.

Before You Go Outside . . .

- Pack this book.
- You might also want to bring a sketchbook or a notebook to write notes about what you see. This can be your *Nature Journal*. Throughout this book you will find prompts about things you can write about in your journal, and ideas for things to sketch. You will need your Nature Journal for most of the suggested activities.
- A few of the activities in this book suggest using the internet to find information. Because sites are always changing, we recommend that kids and grownups explore these resources together. Read more about this on the Resources page 177.
- If you have a cell phone with internet access, consider using an app called iNaturalist that will help you identify and record all the species you observe. You can find more information on the Resources page, 177.

PART 1

Chapter 1

OUR COMMON HOME

Our Homes on Earth

What kind of a home do you live in? There are many kinds of homes. Some homes are small, and some are big. Some homes have a backyard, and some do not. Some homes are in the city, some are in the country, and some are in between. Some of us struggle to find a home, and some of us move around.

The Earth is everybody's home—our ***common home***. *Common* means shared. The Earth is the planet we live on. God created it as a gift for all people. Studying about our world is an important way for us to learn about God and his love for us.

Many Kinds of Creatures

The Earth is home to many kinds of beautiful plants and animals of different sizes, shapes, and colors. Together, the many kinds of living and non-living things on Earth tell us more about God than any one thing tells us by itself. The great variety of living things, or ***organisms***, on Earth is known as ***biodiversity***. The parts of the Earth that support life make up the ***biosphere***. This field book primarily explores plant and animal life.

Differences in organisms exist because those organisms live in many different kinds of homes and natural communities.

Living ***beings***, such as people, plants, and animals, are all God's ***creatures***. Non-living things, such as air, water, rocks, and soil are also God's creatures, because everything has been created by God. In this field book the words *beings*, *things*, and *creatures* all have the same meaning. All three words are used throughout the book. Many Church documents also use these words in this way.

People are special to God. We are created in his image and likeness. We can love, reason with our minds, and choose to do good. Of all the creatures on Earth, only people are called to know and love God.

Saint Josephine Bakhita once said, "I remembered looking at the moon and stars and the beautiful things in nature and saying to myself, 'Who is the master of all these beautiful things?' And I experienced a great desire to see him and know him and honor him. And now I do know him. Thank you, thank you, my God!"[1]

Like Saint Josephine, you may feel amazement when you experience the peace and beauty of nature. You might wonder, *How could God create something so beautiful?* And just imagine—God thinks of you as more marvelous than all of the plants and animals. The human person is his greatest creation of all!

What Is a Biome?

A ***biome*** is a large ***community*** of organisms that includes people, plants, and animals. A biome makes up a large area of the Earth. Within each biome, plants, animals, and other organisms share similar ways of living because they share the same ***climate*** and landscape. Climate is the weather of an area over a long period of time.

Organisms develop changes that help them fit the conditions found in their particular biome. These changes are called ***adaptations***.

This field guide contains chapters about nine biomes found in North America and the islands of Hawaii and Puerto Rico. You probably live in or near one of these biomes.

A **forest** is a community of plants, animals, and other living things that is dominated by trees. Forests are important for people and many kinds of plants, animals, and other organisms. They provide shelter, air, water, food, wood, and medicines. Forests are found where there is enough water moisture to grow trees. We will look at four forest biomes: temperate deciduous forest, coniferous forest, temperate rainforest, and tropical rainforest.

A **grassland** is an area where the plant life is dominated by grasses. Grasslands have few trees, unlike forests, which have many trees. A grassland has enough water moisture to grow grasses and wildflowers, but may not have enough water moisture to grow trees.

A **desert** is a large, dry area of land with thinly scattered plant life. Deserts are found where there is too little water moisture to grow trees and most other plants.

The **tundra** is extremely cold and dry, much like a desert but usually colder.

The **saltwater** or marine biome is composed of the ocean and bays and is the largest biome.

The **freshwater** biome consists of lakes, rivers, streams, and wetlands across the land.

NATURE JOURNAL IDEA

What biome do you live in? How do you know? What biomes would you most like to visit and why?

Ecosystems and Habitats

Indigenous peoples have been a part of the biomes of North America for thousands of years. Their understanding of ecosystems and the plants and animals that live there is called *traditional ecological knowledge*. This knowledge is very important to learning how to care for our common home.

An ***ecosystem*** is a community of living and nonliving beings, together in their environment. There may be many ecosystems in a biome. The non-living parts of an ecosystem are called ***abiotic***, while all living things (even the tiniest) are called ***biotic***. Both biotic and abiotic parts of an ecosystem help to shape it and make it what it is.

Within an ecosystem there are many smaller ***habitats***. A habitat is the place where a person, plant, animal, or other living thing makes its home. Habitats provide shelter, water, food, and space for people and wildlife. Almost every place on Earth, from the hottest deserts to the oceans, is a habitat for some kinds of plants and animals. People too!

When Jesus lived on Earth in the Holy Land, he experienced the subtropical woodland biome. This biome has hot, dry summers and moderate, wet winters. Today the Holy Land is home to many rare plants and animals that thrive there, such as orchids.

In an ecosystem, each organism has a role. This is called a ***niche***. Within an ecosystem many niches fit together like a puzzle. When all organisms and their surrounding environment are healthy and working together, then the puzzle is complete. People and all of God's other creatures need a complete puzzle in order to survive.

Remember, you live in a biome, an ecosystem, *and* a habitat. The biome is the biggest area on Earth that your home is part of, and the habitat is the smallest area, right where you live.

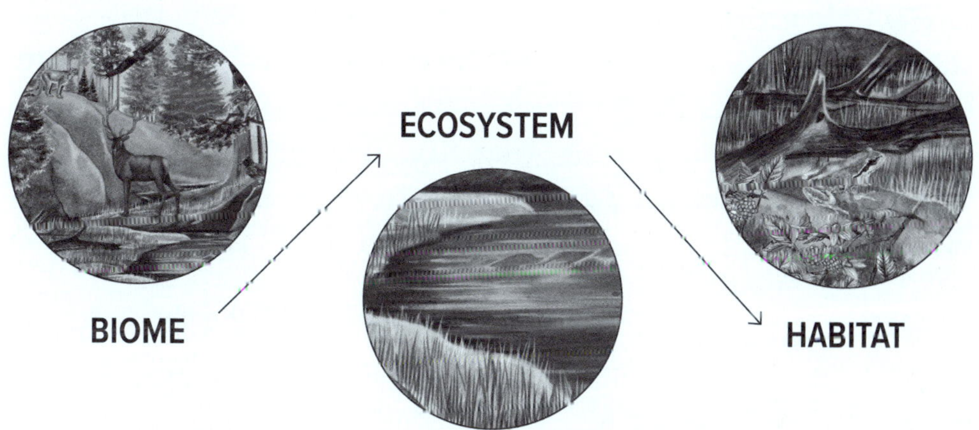

NATURE JOURNAL IDEA

How do you think the climate of the area where Jesus lived affected his life?

Plants, Animals, and Non-Living Things

Plants

Plants make up a large group of organisms. Most of them use sunlight to make their own food. Since they can make their own food, they are called ***producers***. These plants use green matter called ***chlorophyll*** to absorb energy from sunlight into their leaves and stems. In a process called ***photosynthesis*** the plants create food by using sunlight, water, air, and nutrients from the soil, air, or water in which they grow. This food is called ***carbohydrates***.

Trees, shrubs, vines, grasses, vegetables, ferns, and mosses are all plants. Different kinds of plants live in different kinds of habitats.

To make more plants, most plants must create seeds by ***pollination***. Pollination is when a plant's pollen reaches a flower or a cone of the same ***species***, or sometimes a very similar species of plant, to make seeds. Some plants are also able to self-pollinate! This happens when pollen pollinates the same flower or a different flower on the same plant!

A species is a group of living beings that are alike. They can create new life with one another. For example, the corn we eat is a species of plant called *Zea mays*. All the members of a species that live in a community are called a ***population***.

Most flowering plants need insects, animals, and wind to help them pollinate their flowers. Insects and animals serving this purpose are called pollinators. Some kinds of pollinators are bees, butterflies, hummingbirds, and even bats and flies.

Wildflowers grow beneath trees and shrubs in the forest. Some of the most beautiful wildflowers are found in the forest biomes. Like jewels from heaven, they come in all shapes, colors, and sizes, and are important food sources for insects.

Different wildflowers grow in different seasons. Many eye-catching flowers bloom in the spring in ***deciduous*** forests (forests that shed their leaves mostly in the fall) before the trees grow leaves and shade the ground once again.

Did you know that trees can "talk" to each other? In forests, trees have relationships with types of small, organisms called ***fungi***. Research has shown that these fungi, known as mycorrhizae, can pass messages from tree to tree about threats of pests and the health of other trees. Because of this, a forest can almost act like one living organism! God's creatures are so amazing!

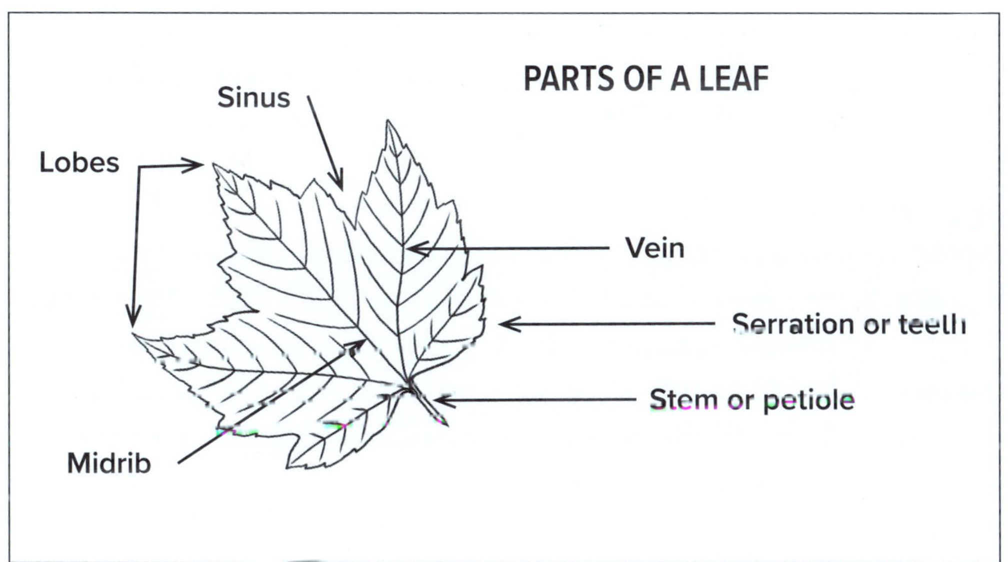

Animals

Animals are a large group of organisms that can move by themselves and cannot make their own food the way green plants do. Animals eat green plants, fungi, and/or other animals. Mammals, birds, reptiles, fish, amphibians, insects, snails, and worms are all animals. Animals are ***consumers***, meaning that to survive they must eat or consume plants or other animals. A consumer can be an ***herbivore***, meaning that it eats plants, or a ***carnivore***, meaning that it eats other animals. Animals that can eat both plants and animals are called ***omnivores***. People are omnivores.

Birds are direct descendants of dinosaurs and are even called ***living dinosaurs*** by scientists!

Animals can be grouped into mammals, birds, arthropods, reptiles, and amphibians.

Mammals are animals that feed milk to their young. Rather than lay eggs, they give birth to their young (except for the platypus and the four spiny anteater species). Many mammals have hair or fur to keep them warm. People are mammals too!

Birds are animals that have wings and feathers. All birds that live today have wings, but they cannot all fly. Also, birds are the only living animals that have feathers! Some bird bones are hollow and full of spaces for air to help them breathe and fly! Birds eat many types of food, like berries, seeds, and insects. Some birds, such as owls and hawks, only eat other animals. Some birds live in the same region all year-round, and others ***migrate***, or travel, to warmer parts of the world during the winter.

Arthropods are a group of animals that includes insects, crabs, and spiders. Arthropods do not have bones like other animals. Rather, they have hard outer shells called ***exoskeletons*** to protect them. They also have segmented bodies. Spiders and insects are both arthropods, but spiders are not insects. Spiders have eight legs, while all kinds of insects have six. Arthropods are very important in the ***web of life*** (the many ways that organisms are connected). For example, they serve as food for many other species of animals, such as birds, mammals, reptiles, and amphibians. The order in which organisms depend on each other for food is called a ***food chain*** or ***food web***.

Specific species of insects cannot survive without certain species of plant. They are dependent on those plants because they have evolved together throughout history. An insect's special plant is called a ***host plant***. Without their host plant, many insects cannot survive. For example, the caterpillars of the endangered Saint Francis' satyr butterfly, named after Saint Francis, feed on a sedge, a grass-like plant. This is why it is important to plant ***native plants***, or plants that evolved over time in certain places, and to protect habitats that already exist.

People need insects too! Insects pollinate many plants: they carry pollen from one plant to another. Pollination allows plants to make fruits and seeds. Without pollination, we would not have the majority of fruits or vegetables we are able to eat.

Reptiles are animals covered in thick scales. Most reptiles lay eggs. You may recognize lizards and turtles as reptiles. Reptiles cannot regulate their own body temperature as you and I do. People have an average temperature of 98.6 degrees, even when it is cold. But a reptile's temperature is determined by the temperature of the air or water that surrounds it. So, if the weather is very cold, their body temperature will be very low.

Amphibians are similar to reptiles in that they are cold blooded. However, most "breathe" through both their lungs and skin. Some amphibians don't have lungs and only breathe through their skin! Most spend time both in water and on land. The majority lay eggs, and their young often go through ***metamorphosis***, like some insects do, to become adults. For example, frogs are amphibians, and when their young hatch from eggs, they must live as tadpoles, swimming in the water for a time before they become frogs that can also live on land.

Did you know that you can help pollinators in your yard? Plant a variety of native flowers of different shapes and sizes. You may want to research which host plants are needed near you. Also, leave an area of small branches and fallen leaves as well as some uncovered areas on the ground to create habitats for pollinators!

In this field guide you will meet some of the different plant and animal species found in each biome. After the common name of each organism, you will see the ***scientific name*** in parenthesis. The scientific name is the same in every language. This helps scientists around the world to communicate with each other about organisms. A scientific name is made of two parts, the generic name and the specific name. The generic name (which begins with a capital letter) tells us what ***genus*** the organism belongs to. A genus is a group of species that are closely related and have similar characteristics. The second part of the scientific name is the species name. Sometimes scientists describe all the species within a genus. When this happens, you will see in parentheses the genus name followed by the abbreviation spp., which means more than one species. Sometimes you will also see a third part added to a scientific name. This describes a subspecies, which is a group or subdivision within a species that has become different from other members of the species, but not different enough to be considered its own species.

Non-living Things

All people, plants, and animals depend on non-living things to survive. God's non-living creatures include water, air, soil, rocks, and sunlight.

In different habitats, non-living things may also be different. For example, shaded habitats are different than sunny habitats. Fresh water is different from salt water. Soil can be different too, depending on what is inside it and how much rain has fallen. Fire is another non-living thing that has an important role in different habitats.

The non-living things in a particular habitat determine what living things, or organisms, can survive there. Organisms develop special ways of dealing with their non-living surroundings, called ***adaptations***. For example, many desert animals can go a long time without drinking water.

In different forests, sunlight, water, soil, and air interact with one another differently. Because of the many trees, sunlight does not always reach the soil. Forests can be shady. In forests, leaves fall and over time create a layer that turns into more soil. The soil is soft and full of life. This kind of soil is ***organic***. Organic material has nutrients for plants to grow. This layer of soil can be thick in some forests, such as the temperate deciduous forest. However, in many tropical rainforests the heavy rains wash away these nutrients. Because of this and other factors, the organic layer might be thin. Many plants in these forests have shallow roots so they can get the nutrients from this soil layer. This is one example of an adaptation in plants caused by their non-living surroundings.

NATURE JOURNAL IDEA

If you look closely, you will see some of the relationships that exist between God's creatures, from the smallest to the largest. These relationships show the beauty and intricacy of God's design. Each relationship is important for the functioning of entire ecosystems, and in turn, of entire biomes. Describe some of the relationships you can see where you live.

PRAYER

Praise is due to you,
  O God, in Zion.
You visit the earth and water it;
  you greatly enrich it;
the river of God is full of water;
  you provide the people with grain,
  for so you have prepared it.
You water its furrows abundantly,
  settling its ridges,
softening it with showers,
  and blessing its growth.

— Psalm 65:1, 9–10

ACTIVITY

Picture Perfect Plants

Did you know that a cell phone application called iNaturalist can help you identify plants and animals in the biome that you live in or visit?

Materials: electronic device, iNaturalist app

Instructions: Have an adult download the iNaturalist app. Now you will be able to take photos of plants and animals to keep. iNaturalist will tell you what kind of species you are observing. Keep a list of every species you see. The app also allows you to see what other people have observed in your area and in the whole world. For this activity, practice taking clear photos of different plants. For each plant, practice taking a picture of the whole plant, a leaf, and if present, a flower. These are different ways to identify plants. You can also join Saint Kateri Conservation Center's "Saint Kateri Annual Catholic Bioblitz" project in iNaturalist! The plants and animals you observe will be added to a list of species observed by Catholics all around the world. Every observation helps the science community know more about biodiversity. You can see more about this app in the Resources page, 177.

Go on a Bug Blitz!

Materials: timer, Nature Journal, pencil

Instructions: Set a timer and count how many different kinds of insects you can find in a minute, ten minutes, or half an hour. Make sure to check under rocks, on flowers, and underneath leaves. Record the number in your Nature Journal. Try it again on a different day and in a different place. You can also take photos of the bugs you find and identify them using iNaturalist.

Chapter 2

THE CREATION OF THE WORLD

Where Did the World Come From?

Have you ever wondered which is true, the creation stories in the Bible or the scientific explanations of the development of life? The answer is . . . both!

Scientific research has discovered that various organisms appeared on the Earth over the course of billions of years. The fossil record shows a picture of these developments throughout time.

The Bible, or ***Sacred Scripture***, is God's word to us. God inspired human authors to write what he wanted to communicate to us, including information about his creation of the world. To understand the Bible, we need to understand the kind of writing of each part, and how it fits in with the whole. There are many facts in the Bible, but not everything in the Bible is meant to be understood as factual. Some stories are symbolic. Some parts of the Bible are poetry. For example, there are two different stories of creation in the first book of the Bible, Genesis. They both tell us that God created the world and people. This is the truth that they tell us. But the two creation stories have different ways of telling us the truth. Let's look at the first story of creation.

NATURE JOURNAL IDEA

Psalm 98 is a prayer of praise to God.

> "O sing to the Lord a new song,
>   for he has done marvelous things . . .
> Let the sea roar, and all that fills it;
>   the world and those who live in it.
> Let the floods clap their hands;
>   let the hills sing together for joy" (Psalm 98:1, 7–8).

Pray these lines, then copy them in your nature journal, or choose one of these other psalms to copy: Psalm 23:1–4, Psalm 42:1–2, Psalm 66:1–4, Psalm 148:1–5

(To learn how to look up a passage in the Bible, see page 184.)

Making Something from Nothing

The first book of the Bible is the Book of Genesis. And the first words of that book are, "In the beginning. . . ."

In the beginning, the Bible tells us, when God created the heavens and the Earth, the Earth was empty and dark, while a wind from God swept over the waters. God said, "Let there be light," and there was light.

The Book of Genesis continues, telling us that God created the waters and the dry land. He created plants and seeds. God created the sun and the moon and the stars. He created fish in the sea and birds in the air. He created animals of every kind. God blessed the animals, saying, "Be fruitful and multiply and fill the waters in the seas, and let birds multiply on the earth" (Genesis 1:22).

The biblical creation stories are not meant to be scientific accounts of what happened. People weren't there yet to make observations! These stories tell us what God wants us to know. They contain very important truths about God himself, about nature, and about human beings. From these Scripture chapters we learn:

- God created everything from nothing, and everything depends on God. God is the source of all that exists.
- Human beings are made in the image and likeness of God.
- All human beings are descended from the first man and woman.
- Men and women have been created with equal dignity.
- God asked human beings to have ***dominion*** over creation. This could be considered our niche. To have dominion means that God wants human beings to take care of creation and to wisely use nature for our needs.

Genesis goes on to say that God made human beings from the dust of the ground and breathed life into us. God created us in his own image. He created us male and female. God said to us, "Be fruitful and multiply, and fill the earth and subdue it; and have dominion over the fish of the sea and over the birds of the air and over every living thing that moves upon the earth" (Genesis 1:28).

God saw everything he had made, and it was very good!

God created more than what we can see in the world. There is more than what we can observe and measure scientifically. There is an invisible ***spiritual world*** that includes our souls, angels, and God. God created angels. An angel is a spirit without a body. Angels have understanding and free will like people do. (Some angels chose to turn against God permanently and became evil spirits, also called demons or devils.) God gives each of us a guardian angel to keep us safe and lead us on the way to heaven.

God created each of us with a ***soul***, which gives life to our body.

Our soul is the spiritual part of us. Our souls are ***immortal***, which means that our souls will never die. Together your body and soul make you, YOU!

God Invites Us to Help

God continues to create and to support his creation at every moment. He also intends for us to help him as his co-workers. God gave us ***dominion*** over the Earth, which means that he entrusted to our care the Earth and all its plants, animals, and non-living things, such as soil and water. He has made us responsible for creation: he asks us to use it for the good of everyone—for the common good.

We Learn from Creation

The *Catechism of the Catholic Church* tells us that the truth, beauty, and goodness of all creatures reflect the greatness of God. We can learn something of what God is like by looking at the vastness and beauty of God's creation (CCC no. 41)! For example, the strength of the wind

God created you as a unity of a body and a soul. BOTH make up you, a unique and loved creation of God. Your physical body expresses you to the world. It is how you can be seen and heard and touched. Your body is truly essential to who you are. It is not possible to separate your body from your soul during your life. The separation of soul and body is what we mean by death. Our soul lives on and our body decays, as all organisms do. But at the end of the world there will be the resurrection of the dead. By his power, God will raise up our bodies, and they will be reunited with our souls forever.

"But ask the animals, and they will teach you; the birds of the air, and they will tell you; ask the plants of the earth, and they will teach you; and the fish of the sea will declare to you. Who among all these does not know that the hand of the Lord has done this?" (Job 12:7–10)

shows God's great power. The ways the microscopic cells in our bodies work together shows God's attention to every detail.

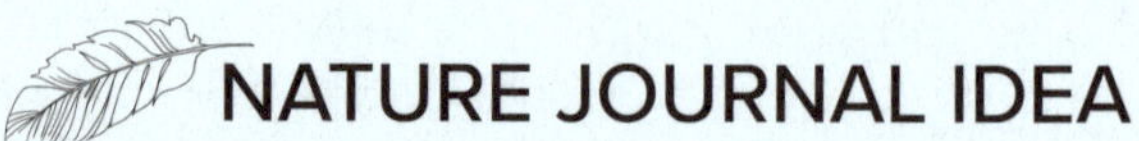

NATURE JOURNAL IDEA

Look at one piece of nature, perhaps something small like a leaf. What does it tell you about God? What does something big, like the ocean, tell you about God?

The First Sin

The Book of Genesis continues with the story of Adam and Eve. God planted a garden in Eden. Out of the ground God made trees and a river to water the garden. God placed Adam and Eve in the garden to take care of it. God asked Adam and Eve not to eat the fruit of one of the trees, the tree of knowledge of good and evil. God wanted them to trust him and obey him freely, out of love. But Adam and Eve disobeyed God and ate the fruit, which broke their friendship with God. When Adam and Eve didn't follow God's will, it was the first ***sin***. This ***original sin*** negatively affects the relationship of human beings with God, with each other, and with all of creation.

NATURE JOURNAL IDEA

What are some examples of these broken relationships that you see in the world today?

PRAYER

"I believe in one God,
the Father almighty,
maker of heaven and earth, of all things visible and invisible . . .
I look forward to the resurrection of the dead and the life of the world to come. Amen."

—From the Nicene Creed

ACTIVITY

Surprise Yourself!

God's creation is surprising and intricate!

Materials: Nature Journal, pencil

Instructions: Go outside and look for the most interesting thing you can find. A green rock? A square seed? Draw or describe it in your Nature Journal.

ACTIVITY

Dig in the Dirt

Materials: Nature Journal, pencil

Instructions: Go to a wooded area. Push aside the leaves on the ground so you can see the dirt. Do you see insects or worms? What else do you see? Is all the soil the same color? Take notes or draw your observations in your Nature Journal.

Chapter 3

JESUS COMES TO EARTH

A New Beginning

Original sin upset God's plan for people to live in love and communion with him and with all creation. But this did not stop God! Jesus came into the world to give human beings a new beginning.

There is only one God, but there are three Persons in God—the Father, the Son, and the Holy Spirit. We call the one God in three Persons the Holy ***Trinity***. The second Person of the Trinity, God the Son, became a man, Jesus. We call this event the ***Incarnation***.

Jesus came to Earth to redeem us from sin and to restore our relationships with God, with each other, and with all of creation. He redeemed us by dying for us on the cross and rising from the dead. The power of Jesus' death and resurrection comes to us through the sacraments that he gave to the Church.

Nature in the Life of Jesus

Jesus was born in Bethlehem and during his life he traveled all around the Holy Land. He walked by the Sea of Galilee to teach, and he called some fishermen to be his apostles. He would often go into the wilderness or up a mountain to pray to his Father. He walked on long, dusty roads to teach and heal people.

NATURE JOURNAL IDEA

There was great biodiversity in the area where Jesus lived! Imagine what Jesus may have thought and felt as he looked at the beautiful plants and animals that he encountered. Can you name any plants or animals that Jesus spoke of in the Bible? (Hint: for starters, see Matthew 10:16, Luke 6:1, Luke 15:4, John 1:48.)

Jesus showed a deep understanding of nature, using plants and animals to teach about God. He told parables, which are stories to make us think. Some of these stories refer to planting seeds, fishing, finding fruit on a tree, or taking care of sheep.

Because he is God, Jesus also showed his power over nature by performing miracles. He calmed a storm. He multiplied bread and fish for a huge crowd. He healed people immediately, and he even brought dead people back to life.

Before he began his ministry, Jesus worked as a carpenter, making things out of wood. But in the Gospel of Luke, Jesus says, "I am the Good Shepherd" (Luke 10:11). So, if he was a carpenter, why did he say he was a shepherd? Jesus uses the image of a shepherd who loves and cares for his sheep to explain how much he loves and cares for us.

NATURE JOURNAL IDEA

Jesus used the example of birds to teach us to trust in God and not to worry about things. He said, "Look at the birds of the air; they neither sow nor reap nor gather into barns, and yet your heavenly Father feeds them. Are you not of more value than they?" (Matthew 6:26). What are some of the ways that God takes care of you?

Jesus Uses Nature in the Sacraments

Jesus chose to use things found in creation—water, oil, wheat, grapes—for the sacraments. For example, water is used in Baptism. Oil is used in Holy Orders and the Anointing of the Sick. Most importantly, wheat and grapes are used to make the bread and wine that become the Body and Blood of Jesus Christ in the sacrament of the Eucharist. At Mass we receive the Body of Christ in Holy Communion, which nourishes and strengthens us.

Did you know that the chalice and other cups that hold the Eucharist at Mass must be washed in a special sink called the ***sacrarium***, where all the water drains directly into the Earth?

As Jesus was going back to heaven, he said to his apostles, "Go into all the world and proclaim the good news to the whole creation" (Mark 16:15). Now Jesus sends us to share the good news that he came to save us from sin and restore our friendship with God.

Jesus Gives Us the Path to Follow

When someone asked Jesus what was the most important commandment, Jesus answered, "'You shall love the Lord your God with all your heart, and with all your soul, and with all your mind.' This is the greatest and first commandment. And a second is like it: 'You shall love your neighbor as yourself'" (Matthew 22:37–39).

Love for God leads to love for our "neighbor," which really means all human beings. Caring for our common home is essential to loving our neighbor. Everyone needs a healthy environment.

Jesus gives us the grace we need to be able to live this love of God and neighbor. We receive this grace through the sacraments, especially Baptism, Confirmation, the Eucharist, and Reconciliation.

NATURE JOURNAL IDEA

Bring your Bible outside and read. You can read one of these passages or another of your choosing: Genesis 1, Psalm 23, Psalm 111, Isaiah 25:6–9, or Luke 5:1–11.

Thomas Merton was an American monk and a famous author. He once wrote in his journal, "By the reading of Scripture I am so renewed that all nature seems renewed around me and with me. The sky seems to be a pure, a cooler blue, the trees a deeper green . . . the whole world is charged with the glory of God, and I feel fire and music in the earth under my feet."[2]

PRAYER

God of Life, creation softly whispers truths about your nature through its beauty and mystery. Inspire me to marvel at the beautiful mysteries of nature, to draw me to the most profound mystery of all—the Incarnation.[3]

—Jodyanne Benson

ACTIVITY

Scripture and Stargazing Party

Did you know that there is a meteor shower that is named after a saint? St. Lawrence's Tears is a meteor shower that occurs every year at the end of July and can be seen on the saint's feast day on August 10. If you can, organize your stargazing party for Saint Lawrence's feast day or in celebration of a different feast day!

Materials: blankets to lie on, snacks, flashlight, Bible

Instructions: With your grown-up's permission, invite friends and family to gaze at the stars and to reflect on Scripture. If you can, do this outside in an open space. You can spread out blankets or set up chairs for your invites. Find Matthew 2:9–11 in your Bible. (If you need help locating this Scripture passage, see page 184.) Read the Scripture out loud with the help of your flashlight. You may want to read the passage more than once. Share what stood out to you in this passage and ask others what stood out to them. Then continue gazing at the beautiful stars God created!

Grow a Modern Mustard Plant

Jesus speaks about the mustard seed, and how small it is. The Jerusalem mustard seed is especially small! Did you know that mustard plants have been changed by people over the years to develop some of the vegetables we see today? Brussels sprouts, broccoli, kale, and cabbage all come from the original wild mustard seed. Ask your parents to buy one or more of these types of vegetables.

Materials: Nature Journal, pencil, brussels sprouts, broccoli, kale and/or cabbage, container partially filled with water, a device with internet access (optional).

Instructions: First observe your vegetable and draw or describe it in your nature journal. What does it taste like? If you have more than one kind, describe how these vegetables are alike and how they are different. Some plants don't need seeds to grow: you can place specific scraps of the vegetable in water. This can be done with all the vegetables in this activity that come from the mustard seed. For example, a brussels sprout can be placed on the top of a bottle (or any container) that is filled with water. Make sure just the cut end of the brussels sprout is touching the water: eventually it should grow roots. Research how your own vegetable(s) can grow this way and try it!

Chapter 4

THE CHURCH TEACHES ABOUT ECOLOGY

Jesus established the Church to continue his work on Earth. The twelve apostles of Jesus became the first bishops, and Peter became their head, the first pope. The pope and bishops of today all trace themselves back to the twelve apostles.

The Church continues to teach as Jesus did, and to celebrate the sacraments that Jesus gave us. The importance of our role in taking care of the Earth and studying the natural world has been a part of Church teaching throughout history.

Catholic Social Teaching

Our faith teaches us that we are all connected. Humans and the rest of God's creation depend on one another for survival, and relationships between humans and God, humans and one another, and humans and nature are very important. To make sure these relationships are healthy, the Church gives us the principles of ***Catholic social teaching.*** Catholic social teaching guides us in our relationships with each other and with all of creation. *Social* means people talking, working, and playing with each other. Catholic social teaching helps us understand that what we do affects the whole human family. It teaches us to make good decisions that help each other and the Earth.

The Seven Themes of Catholic Social Teaching

1. God made each one of us. He loves us. Every human life is important and must be protected.
2. God made each of us part of a family and part of a community to help each other.
3. God gave us rights and responsibilities so that everyone has the opportunity to live a safe, healthy, and good life. You have a *right* to things that are just. For example, you have a right to life.
4. God wants us to help people who are poor or weak, bullied, or mistreated.
5. When we go to school or to work, we are cooperating with God's work. Workers, students, and teachers should be treated fairly and with respect.
6. All of us make up one human family of sisters and brothers who must love each other. We are to support each other.
7. The world is made by God and is sustained (supported) by him. We should take care of all of God's creation, including people, plants, animals, air, water, soil, sand, and rocks.[4]

The Teaching of Recent Popes

Since the time of Saint Peter, the popes have continued Jesus' teaching. Three recent popes have been especially committed to care for creation as an important aspect of social justice.

Saint John Paul II

Pope John Paul II, originally from Poland, was one of the greatest popes of our Church. He is now a saint! Pope John Paul II spoke about the importance of understanding the human person as made up of body and soul. He was very concerned about marriage and family life. He traveled around the world (to 129 countries) to teach and to show his concern for people everywhere. Pope John Paul II called for an "***ecological conversion***."[5] This means a change of heart in the way we think and act that will help us to live in harmony with God, people, and all of nature. He felt it was good that many more people were coming to understand the importance of taking care of our planet Earth according to the plan of our Creator.

Pope Benedict XVI

Pope Benedict XVI is known as "the Green Pope," because he spoke so well and often about caring for creation. Pope Benedict was born in Germany and was a great teacher. He said, "The family needs a home. . . . For the human family, this home is the earth, the environment that God the Creator has given us to inhabit with creativity and responsibility. We need to care for the environment."[6]

Pope Francis

Pope Francis was born in Argentina. He wrote a special letter to the world asking people to protect our common home, the Earth. This letter is called ***Laudato Si'***.[7] (It is an Italian phrase that means "Praise to God.") Like Saint Francis of Assisi, the Holy Father reminds us that our common home is like a sister with whom we share our life and a beautiful mother who opens her arms to hug us.

Pope Francis asks us to care about pollution, climate change, clean water; the many species on Earth (biodiversity); the quality of human life; and people who are poor or mistreated.

NATURE JOURNAL IDEA

Think about what these three popes had to say about the importance of ecology. Write a letter to your family, class, or community. What would you say to encourage others to take care of our common home?

Saints of the Church

A ***saint*** is a holy person, one who loved God in an amazing way on Earth and is now in heaven. Some of these people have been canonized (officially declared to be in heaven), but everyone else in heaven is a saint, too. We can ask saints to ***intercede*** for us. To intercede is to pray for the sake of someone else. The intercession of the saints is when they ask God for graces on our behalf.

Remember that you are called to become a saint too! In words and actions, the saints have much to teach us about caring for the environment.

The ***communion of saints*** is the sharing of God's grace among all members of his Church. This includes people on Earth, souls in ***purgatory***, and the saints in heaven. Purgatory is where souls go to be cleansed before entering heaven. We should pray for souls in purgatory.

Communion means sharing. When we share what we can see, and also share what we cannot see—love, prayers, and the graces and spiritual riches of God—we are being active members of the communion of saints.

Saint Thérèse of Lisieux

Saint Thérèse is a ***Doctor of the Church***, meaning that she is a great teacher in the communion of saints. Thérèse lived in France at the end of the nineteenth century. She wrote about nature to teach us about the love that God has for us. She wrote about springtime beauty, flowers, meadows, trees, mountains, the sea, sunshine, and the stars at night. She called these creations of God the ***book of nature***. Saint Thérèse wrote: "Jesus set before me the book of nature. I understood how all the flowers he created are beautiful, how the splendor of the rose and the whiteness of the lily do not take away the perfume of the little violet or the delightful simplicity of the daisy. . . . Perfection consists in doing his will, in being what he wills us to be."[8]

NATURE JOURNAL IDEA

Pope Francis mentions Saint Thérèse in *Laudato Si'* because of her commitment to doing small actions with love.[9] What are some small actions you can take today to help the natural world around you?

Saint Hildegard of Bingen

Saint Hildegard is also a Doctor of the Church. She lived during the twelfth century in Germany. She is known for her love of God, studies of the natural world, poetry, and music. She was very interested in ***botany***, the study of plants. She was a nun and used plants and other natural sources to help other nuns when they were sick. Hildegard taught us that our Christian way of life is a path to living in community with all of creation. Saint Hildegard wrote, "God, who made

A novena is a Catholic practice of praying for something nine days in a row. This tradition comes from when the early Christians prayed for the nine days between the Ascension of Jesus and the coming of the Holy Spirit on Pentecost. You can make a novena by praying to a saint for the nine days before his or her feast day.

all things by his will, created them so that his name would be known and glorified, showing in them not just the things that are visible and temporal, but also the things that are invisible and ***eternal***."[10] Here, Saint Hildegard tells us how creation can show us more about ourselves and about God, who is eternal, which means having no beginning or end.

NATURE JOURNAL IDEA

Saint Thérèse and Saint Hildegard often used nature as an inspiration in their writings. Both of these saints compared people to flowers. If you could compare yourself to a kind of flower or another plant, which one would you choose and why?

PRAYER

Saint Thérèse said she wanted to use her time in heaven doing good on Earth. She even said that she would shower roses down from heaven. (This refers to her help, but can also be an actual rose!) Pray for the intercession of Saint Thérèse for the good that you want to do today. Here is a prayer you can use:

> O Little Thérèse of the Child Jesus, please pick for me a rose from the heavenly garden and send it to me as a message of love. O Little Flower of Jesus, ask God to grant the favors I now place with confidence in your hands (mention your special prayer request here). Saint Thérèse, help me to always believe, as you did, in God's great love for me, so that I may imitate your "little way" each day. Amen.

Make Native Plant Greenhouses

Many native plant seeds need winter to germinate in the spring.

Materials: seeds of a few kinds of plants, one or more plastic milk jugs, strong scissors, a nail, dirt or potting soil, masking or duct tape, marker, an adult to help you do the cutting and hole punching safely.

Instructions: In the winter, collect plastic milk jugs and remove the lids. Cut them in half partway, so that the top half of each jug is still connected, but can be folded over, so you can fill the bottom with dirt. Ask a parent to help you use the nail to make holes in the bottoms! Fill the bottom half of each jug with dirt and place the seeds in the dirt. Flip the top halves back on, tape them shut, and label them. Place them outside. They will become greenhouses where plants will germinate in the spring!

Pray the Stations of the Cross Outdoors

The Stations of the Cross is a Catholic tradition that dates back to the early times in Jerusalem when people would walk to holy places to remember Jesus' crucifixion. Today, Catholic churches have pictures that depict the day Jesus died. These are set up as stations, and we can pray at each one. Some churches have these stations outside so that people can pray the stations in nature.

Materials: Stations of the Cross pictures and prayers, printed from an online source or drawn by hand; tape, twine, or rocks to fasten the stations outside.

Instructions: Draw or print out the stations on pieces of paper or card stock and place them in order outside. You can tape or tie them to trees, or to garden objects, or flat on a path (anchored with rocks). Now pray the Stations of the Cross as you spend time in nature! At each station you can think about how Jesus must have felt or recite the prayer that goes with the picture.

Chapter 5

Saint Kateri Tekakwitha

We can ask any saint to pray for us, but some saints have special connections to certain needs or topics. We say that a certain saint is the ***patron saint*** of that need or topic. Saint Kateri Tekakwitha[*] is the patron saint of Indigenous peoples and also the patron of care for creation.

> ***Indigenous*** refers to a group of people who have lived in a place for many generations, sometimes for thousands of years. Native Americans, the Indigenous peoples of North America, have a traditional knowledge of ecology that is passed on by word of mouth from adults to children, one generation after another.

Tekakwitha was born in 1656 in what is now upstate New York, U.S.A. She grew up there and later lived in what is now the province of Quebec, Canada. Tekakwitha's mother was Algonquin, and her father was Haudenosaunee[†] from the Kanien'kehá:ka[‡] (also known as Mohawk) tribe. Both of these groups are Indigenous nations of North America.

The name Tekakwitha means "One who places things in order" or "To put everything in place."

---

[*] Usually pronounced Tek-ah-KWEETH-ah. The Mohawk pronunciation is Day-gah-KWEE-dah.

[†] Pronounced Hoe-dee-no-SHOW-nee.

[‡] Pronounced Gahn-yin-gay-HA-gah.

When Tekakwitha was four years old, there was an outbreak of smallpox in her village. Her parents and her little brother died from the illness, and her aunt and uncle took her into their family and raised her. Although Tekakwitha had survived the smallpox, her face was scarred, and her eyesight was poor. She often wore a blanket over her head to shade her eyes from the bright sun.

In many ways, Tekakwitha lived just the way other young Mohawk girls lived. She helped grow corn, beans, and squash in the fields. She collected wood in the forest and carried a homemade container of water from a spring. She helped clean the longhouse in which her family lived. Tekakwitha was very good with her hands and made beautiful clothing and jewelry with beads.

Eastern box turtles (*Terrapene carolina carolina*) are an important symbol for many Indigenous people. Some use turtle shells as rattles during ceremonial dances. Saint Kateri Tekakwitha was a member of the Mohawk Turtle Clan. Other Haudenosaunee clans include Bear, Wolf, Snipe, Deer, Beaver, Heron, Hawk, and Eel.

Living in the forest, she knew a lot about the natural world around her. For many years her people had lived closely with the plants and animals of the forests, grasslands, fields, lakes, and rivers. Like all other Indigenous people, they fished, hunted, farmed, and gathered what they needed for food, clothing, and shelter.

Tekakwitha's mother had been Catholic, and Tekakwitha became interested in Catholicism while listening to the three priests who visited her village. She was baptized on Easter Sunday in 1676 when she was nineteen years old. She took the name Kateri,* which is a form of Katherine, after Saint Catherine of Siena.

* Usually pronounced Kuh-TAIR-ee or CAT-er-ee. The Mohawk pronunciation is GAH-dah-lee or Gah-deh-LEE.

Some of the people in her village bullied Kateri because of her Catholic faith. They did not understand her love of Jesus. They called her names and threw rocks at her. Because of this, when she could, Kateri left her village. With friends, she traveled north on foot and by canoe through woods and over mountains to live in a community with other Catholic Indigenous people in the area now known as Quebec Province, Canada.

NATURE JOURNAL IDEA

Kateri always remembered to give thanks to God for all the people and good things in her life. Giving thanks is an important part of many Indigenous traditions. Write a list of everything you can think of that you are thankful for.

In her new community, Kateri went to Mass often, sometimes every day. She taught prayers to children and helped people who were sick or old. People around her said she was a holy woman.

Saint Kateri was well known for her love of Jesus. It is said that she would ask, “Who will teach me what is most pleasing to God, so I may do it?”

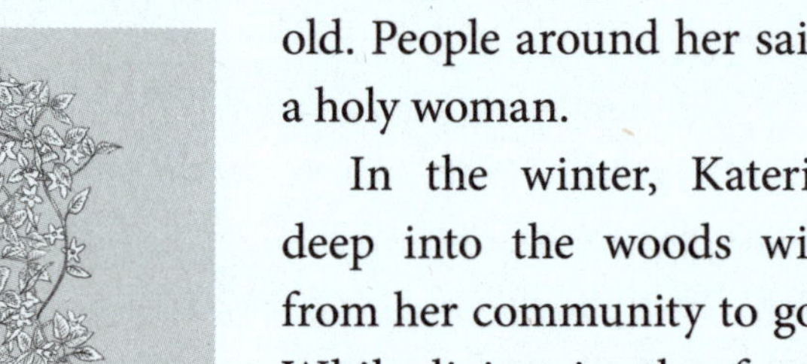

In the winter, Kateri traveled deep into the woods with others from her community to go hunting. While living in the forest, Kateri prayed in front of crosses she made out of tree branches. Later, Kateri decided to stay closer to home and the chapel she loved, even if it meant she would be hungry during the long winters.

Kateri died from a serious illness in 1680, when she was twenty-four years old.

You can visit the places where Kateri lived, such as the Saint Kateri National Shrine in Fonda, New York, and the Shrine of Our Lady of Martyrs in Auriesville, New York. Saint Kateri is buried in Kahnawake,

Quebec, at the St. Francis Xavier Mission. In the United States, Saint Kateri's feast day is celebrated on July 14. In Canada, her day is April 17.

NATURE JOURNAL IDEA

Write a prayer asking Saint Kateri to intercede for you to God.

PRAYER

Sit in a quiet place outdoors. Make the Sign of the Cross, then pray:

"I praise you, Lord, for ______________________________," filling in something for which you want to praise God. Finish with "Amen" and the Sign of the Cross.

ACTIVITY

Make a Cross out of Sticks

Saint Kateri would often make crosses out of sticks to help her in prayer. The cross reminded her of the great love Jesus showed by dying on the cross for us.

Materials: two sticks (one shorter, one longer), a long stem of green grass, or a thin vine, or twine (about one to two feet long).

Instructions: Carefully tear off the grass blades or leaves from the stem or vine. Place the two sticks in the shape of a cross. Leave a few inches of the stem or vine free (to make a knot when you finish). Wrap the stem or vine around the crossed part of the sticks, switching directions partway through, so that the stem or vine will make an "X" around the middle of the crossed sticks. Leave a few inches free at the end, and tie both ends together to hold the sticks. Knot the stem or vine a few times in order to hold the sticks together well.

Use your cross to give thanks and say a prayer to God! You can also ask Saint Kateri to say a prayer for you!

ACTIVITY

Create a Wayside Shrine

Throughout history, people have made wayside shrines—small boxes or tiny houses containing items devoted to a saint, Mary, or Jesus. Wayside shrines are placed beside roads or trails. You can make a shrine at home, in your yard, at your parish, or at school. These shrines remind people of the Lord and our community of saints.

Materials: small rock, paint, paintbrush (or a laminated prayer card or garden statue of Jesus, Mary, or a saint), sticks or four larger, flat rocks to build a small house for the image, natural items like shells, flowers, seeds, pebbles

Instructions: Paint an image of Jesus, Mary, or a favorite saint on a small, smooth rock. This rock must be small enough to go inside your shrine. (If you want to use an image that you already have, make sure that it is made of a material that will not be damaged by the weather.) You may want to construct your shrine along a fence or at the base of a tree between the roots. This will help give it stability. Make three walls and a roof using your rocks or sticks. Then place your painted rock or image inside the shrine. Finally, decorate the shrine with the natural items you have. You can even use the cross of sticks from the previous activity. Make sure to take a photo!

Chapter 6

SAINT FRANCIS OF ASSISI

Saint Francis of Assisi is one of the most popular saints of the Church. He is another patron saint of ecology, like Saint Kateri. He is also the patron saint of animals and of the country of Italy.

Francis was born in Assisi, Italy, more than eight hundred years ago. One day, he had a vision in which Jesus asked him to repair his Church. Francis repaired an old church called San Damiano. Later, Francis realized that God was asking him to help repair something much bigger—the Church made up of all people who believed in Jesus.

Francis began to live a life of penance, desiring to turn his life over completely to God. He showed that he was a penitent (a person doing penance) by wearing a rough robe and begging for his food. He gave away all his possessions to the poor. He spent time praying in church and also out in the woods. Other men joined him because they wanted to give their lives to God, too. They lived together as brothers.

Francis and his brothers spoke to everyone to encourage them to come back to Jesus. Eventually more and more people began to live better lives. He and his brothers traveled throughout Italy and beyond, preaching to encourage people to return to the Church and become good followers of Jesus. Francis helped the sick and taught about living simple and poor lives, relying more on the gifts of God than on worldly goods. The brothers begged for what they needed to live and passed the rest of what they received to other people who were poor.

One of the followers of Saint Francis wrote about the instructions Francis gave to the brother tending the vegetable garden. Francis said to leave the edges of the garden untouched so that wildflowers could grow there. He said that their beauty would remind others of God. Francis also told the gardener to use part of the vegetable garden to plant beautiful and fragrant flowers. That way, people would see the flowers' beauty and praise God for it. What flower reminds you the most of God? Write about it in your Nature Journal.

One day while Francis and his brothers were walking, Francis looked up and saw the trees full of birds. Francis ran toward the birds and humbly asked them to listen to the word of God. "My brothers, birds," Francis said, "you should praise your Creator very much and always love him; he gave you feathers to clothe you, wings so that you can fly, and whatever else was necessary for you."[11] The birds stretched their necks and extended their wings as Francis walked by them, blessing them. From that day on, Francis encouraged all creatures to praise and love their Creator.

Whenever Francis would gaze at the sky or the smallest of animals, he would burst into song to praise God. He even invited flowers, rocks, and fields to praise the Lord. He would call all creatures, no matter how small, by the name of *brother* or *sister.* Even the wind and the water were his brother and sister.

NATURE JOURNAL IDEA

How do you think birds can praise God, their creator? How can flowers? How can you? What is the difference between how you can praise God and how animals or plants can?

Saint Francis is an inspiration to many people of faith, so much so that people have devoted their entire lives to Christ through Francis' way of life. They are called Franciscans. Pope Francis took the name Francis after Saint Francis of Assisi.

NATURE JOURNAL IDEA

Write a prayer of praise to God, your Creator.

Saint Francis is well known for the Canticle of the Creatures. Written late in the saint's life, when blindness had limited his sight of the world, the song shows his great love for God, people, and the whole of creation. The title of Pope Francis' encyclical, Laudato Si', is a direct quote from this canticle (song).

Saint Francis' feast day is October 4. We ask him to pray for us.

PRAYER

Canticle of the Creatures

Praised be you, my Lord, with all your creatures,
especially Sir Brother Sun,
who is the day, and through whom you give us light.
He is beautiful and radiant with great splendor,
and bears a likeness of you, Most High One.
Praised be you, my Lord, through Sister Moon and the stars;
in heaven you formed them clear and precious and beautiful.
Praised be you, my Lord, through Brother Wind,
and through the air, cloudy and serene, and every kind of weather,
through whom you give sustenance to your creatures.

Praised be you, my Lord, through Sister Water,
who is very useful and humble and precious. [12]

—Saint Francis

ACTIVITY

Identify Bird Songs

No doubt you've heard many different kinds of bird songs. Some bird songs can be written out to help us to know what kind of bird they are. For example, the Carolina Wren says, "tea kettle tea kettle."

Materials: Nature Journal, pencil

Instructions: Go outside and listen. What kind of bird song do you hear? Write out what it sounds like to you. Do you know what species of bird sings this song? You can research more about the bird you chose and how it was named. Write it all down in your Nature Journal.

ACTIVITY

Bless Your Pets or Garden

Materials: a Bible; the blessing prayer; a treat for each pet; optional treats for the people who attend, such as candy, cookies, or fruit.

Instructions: Before the event, find a passage to read from the Bible (for example, Genesis 1:24–25, Genesis 1:27–28, Psalm 104:24, or Psalm 36:5–6.) Write a short blessing prayer or use this one: "God our Creator, thank you for the gift of all the creatures of the Earth. We especially thank you for our pets, who bring us joy and remind us of your love for us. Please take care of our pets and give them a long, happy life. Amen."

Invite your family or friends to attend. Gather near your pets (outside if your pet can go outside). Ask everyone to be quiet, and then read a passage from the Bible, and pray the prayer asking God to bless the pets. You can finish by having everyone pray the Our Father. Then give your pets a treat. If you like, give the people who attend treats as well.

No pets? No problem! You can also organize a blessing for your garden, even if it is a small indoor herb garden. Consider making people treats with at least one ingredient from your garden!

PART 2

Chapter 7

Our Home in the Temperate Deciduous Forest

Temperate deciduous forests have many broad-leaved trees that shed all their leaves during one season. ***Temperate*** means moderate, or in the middle. Temperate biomes are midway between hot and cold biomes. ***Deciduous*** means that the trees' leaves fall off seasonally.

The deciduous forest has a temperate climate with a winter season and year-round precipitation (rain and snow). There are four seasons, with warm summers, wet springs, colorful falls (autumns), and cold winters, often with snow.

From top to bottom, a mature temperate deciduous forest can have four or more layers. The tops of tall trees form the forest ***canopy***. Below the canopy is the ***understory***, which has smaller species of trees and younger trees that are not full grown. The shrub layer is next, with its woody bushes, shrubs, and brambles. Below this is the ***herb layer***, consisting of herbaceous plants. Herbs are soft-stemmed plants and include wildflowers, ferns, and grasses.

Plants of the Temperate Deciduous Forest

You will find many types of trees, shrubs, and herbs (wildflowers, ferns, and grasses) in the forest. Trees in this type of forest have many different shapes, with unique leaves and seeds. Most of these trees turn colors in the fall. Deciduous forests also have evergreen trees with needle-like leaves. Some of the most beautiful wildflowers are found in the forest. Like jewels

Birch trees have a thick white or gray-brown waterproof bark that is used by some Native American tribes to line the outside of canoes.

from heaven, they come in all shapes, colors, and sizes, and are important food sources for insects. Various wildflowers grow in the seasons that have the right climate for them. Some flowers bloom in the spring and last a short time. They are called spring ***ephemerals***.

White oak (*Quercus alba*) White oak trees are deciduous trees with long, broad leaves that have seven to nine ***lobes*** (rounded parts) in each leaf. The bark of a mature white oak is a light ashy gray color and usually has rectangular ridges. White oaks are often used for wood. They were even used in ships before steel was available. These are one of the most important types of trees in a forest! This is why the white oak is often part of ***reforestation*** efforts, which is the practice of planting trees in an area where they have been removed. Their nuts, called acorns, are full of nutrients and are excellent food for birds and mammals, such as woodpeckers, squirrels, and deer. The white oak and other oaks are also host plants for butterflies, including duskywings and hairstreaks. Butterflies lay eggs on oak leaves and their caterpillars eat the leaves!

Natural forest fires are important ways that dead branches are cleaned out of a forest and the soil is restored. Natural fires start from lightning storms and dry conditions. If there have been no natural fires for many years, people might use prescribed fire to help the cleaning process. "Prescribed fire" means a planned fire that is good for the forest. However, when people accidentally start a fire by being careless, that fire may cause great damage to a forest and destroy homes.

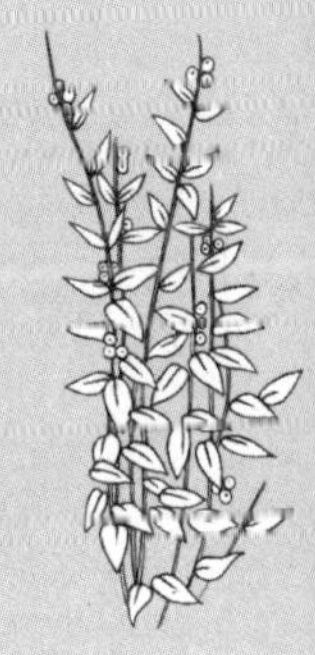

Eastern white pine (*Pinus strobus*) Pine trees are evergreens with needle-like leaves. Pine needles do not fall off the tree all in one season like deciduous trees. The eastern white pine has five needles per bundle. Pine trees make cones containing seeds that provide food for birds and other animals. A mature eastern white pine tree has reddish-brown or grayish brown bark with long, rounded ridges.

Saint Kateri knew a lot about the white pine tree. That kind of tree was a symbol of peace and unity for her tribal nation, the Haudenosaunee. Native Americans ate the inner bark for food in the winter and made a drink of steeped pine needles that contained high levels of vitamin C.

NATURE JOURNAL IDEA

Trees are often identified by the shape of their leaves, but they can also be identified by the kind of bark that they have. This is especially helpful when deciduous trees have lost their leaves. Bark protects trees from other organisms like insects and it also helps the tree keep the right amount of moisture and heat. Smooth bark best protects trees from insects, but it takes longer to grow. Cracked bark may provide a habitat for insects that can harm a tree, but it also grows faster. Go outside and record the types of bark you see in your nature journal. You may want to bring a crayon (take off the paper) and use the side of it to make bark rubbings in your journal.

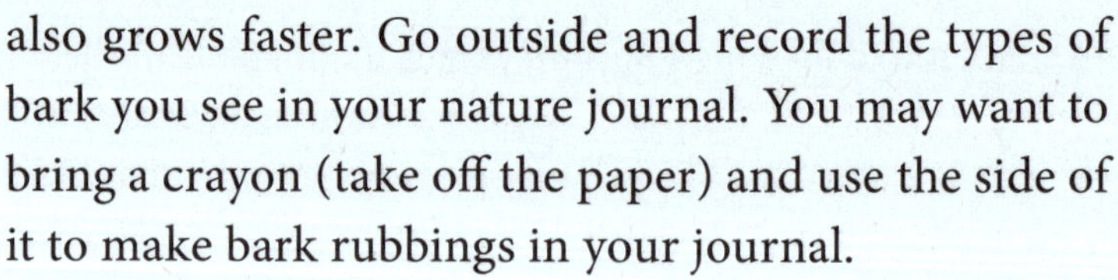

Spicebush (*Lindera benzoin*) The deciduous shrub called spicebush is an important part of a forest. It is the host for the spicebush swallowtail, a beautiful black butterfly. If you squish a spicebush leaf, you will smell a sweet and spicy smell. In the spring, spicebush has small yellow flowers that attract ***pollinators***, organisms that help to move pollen between flowers. Spicebushes produce small berries that birds and mammals like to eat.

Spring beauty (*Claytonia* spp.) The spring beauty is a pink and white wildflower that is found in forest clearings in almost every state. In different places this plant may look different. This plant's roots grow in ***tubers*** like a potato. Native American people ate them. This flower is especially important to bees.

Saint Mother Theodore Guerin

Originally from France, Mother Theodore became a religious sister, and in 1840 she came to the United States as a missionary. She only lived another sixteen years, but during that time she opened schools, orphanages, and pharmacies where the poor people could get free medicine. Some of the medicine came from native plants, such as the cone flower and the leaves and flowers of the linden tree. The stained glass windows at her shrine at Saint Mary-of-the-Woods, Indiana, show some of the plants she used to help the sick.

Animals of the Temperate Deciduous Forest

Many animals make their home in the temperate deciduous forest. The moisture and shade make the forest a comfortable place for various species to live.

Arthropods of the Temperate Deciduous Forest

Arthropods make up seventy percent of the species in a forest. That means there are more types of arthropods than any other animal in the forest! Arthropods are extremely important in the web of life because they provide food for other animals and they pollinate plants, which in turn make more plants and therefore more food! Without arthropods, people and animals would not survive.

Tiger beetle (*Cicindela and Megacephala* spp.) Tiger beetles are ***predators***, meaning they kill and eat other animals. Their ***prey***, that is, the organisms that they kill to eat, are insects and other arthropods. They help keep ecosystems and gardens healthy. They have long legs and big eyes that make them great hunters like their namesake, the tiger. Like most beetles, they have two sets of wings. Keep your eyes peeled—these beetles are fast! You can find them running along hiking trails and along the forest edge. Tiger beetles can be many different colors, including bright, metallic green.

Daddy longlegs (*Leiobunum aldrichi*) This anthropod has long legs and a tiny body. You have probably gone into the woods or your yard and seen a daddy longlegs walking across the bark of a tree. Do not be afraid! These spider-like arthropods will not hurt you. The daddy longlegs is not a spider; it is a harvestman. A harvestman may look like a spider, but some parts of its body are different. It likes to hide in the bark of trees. Daddy longlegs are ***omnivores***, which means that they eat both plants and animals. They eat insects, fungi, also called funguses, and even bird poop! They also are an important source of food for birds, although sometimes one will escape by losing a leg. The next time you see a daddy longlegs, let it go on its way to see another day!

Mason bee (*Osmia lignaria*) Mason bees are a special kind of native bee. They use wet mud to create a place to lay their eggs! Mason bees are a gentle bee and do not sting. (Even bees that do sting only sting when they are scared or threatened.) The mason bee lives alone, not in a colony, so it is called a solitary bee. Mason bees are important for pollination. They can visit up to 2,500 flowers a day! They pollinate fruit and nut trees in orchards. Mason bees pollinate many flowers that bloom in the spring, like the spring beauty. If you go out in your yard after a rain, you might find mason bees collecting a little mud from the ground and carrying it away.

Saint John the Baptist

Saint John the Baptist is an important person in the Gospels. (You can read about him in all four Gospels. See, for example, Luke 3:1–20.) His job was to prepare the world for Jesus, and he did this by urging people to be sorry for their sins. He baptized them in the Jordan River as a sign of their repentance (sorrow and desire to change). John was very close to nature. He spent his days in the wilderness, where he ate locusts and wild honey.

Birds of the Temperate Deciduous Forest

Deciduous forest birds eat seeds from many types of trees, as well as insects that live inside the trees. Forest birds are adapted to survive in shaded environments. Many forest birds nest or find shelter in cavities, or holes in trees. Others nest in the branches of trees and shrubs. Some forest birds spend all winter and summer in the same forest. Other birds, such as warblers, are visitors from other places and migrate during different seasons.

Broad-winged hawk (*Buteo platypterus*) The broad-winged hawk is a bird about the size of a crow. These hawks make their nests in deciduous and mixed forests. They have long tails with black and white stripes. Many migrate over 4,000 miles in the fall to warmer areas in Central and South America! They travel in large groups called kettles. This is one example of how different biomes are connected to one another.

Carolina wren (*Thryothorus ludovicianus*) Carolina wrens are tiny brown birds that you may see flitting in a forest. Their tails stand straight up as they hop from branch to branch. Their curved bills are built to pluck small insects and spiders from branches. This little wren is found in the northeastern and southeastern U.S. These wrens are secretive; if you are not paying attention, you may not see them! But you can certainly hear them and learn their call. Wrens have beautiful songs that can be heard from far away.

NATURE JOURNAL IDEA

The next time you hear a bird singing, think of it as a sweet whisper of Jesus Christ's love for you. What prayer might you sing back?

Bird songs are among the most beautiful sounds on Earth. They are longer and more complex than any of the other sounds birds make. Songs can be mournful, cheerful, or eerie, but they are all about love! Birds mainly sing to find mates. The wood thrush (*Hylocichla mustelina*) is a brown robin-like bird that lives in eastern deciduous forests. Despite its drab color, its song (EE-oh-LAY) has been called the most beautiful birdsong in all of North America!

Mammals of the Temperate Deciduous Forest

Mammals living in the temperate deciduous forest are adapted to use the many seeds and leaves that trees provide. Because there is a diversity of seeds, there are many types of smaller animals in forests, such as many species of chipmunks, squirrels, and mice. There are also larger animals, such as bobcats, foxes, black bears, deer, and moose. Each mammal has its own niche in the forest ecosystem.

White-tailed deer (*Odocoileus virginianus*) The white-tailed deer is an important part of this ecosystem. These deer live on the forest edge and are generalists, eating grasses, shoots, and other plants. They provide food for people, cougars, wolves, and other predators. Deer are quiet animals and are a peaceful sight in the woods.

Red fox (*Vulpes vulpes*) Red foxes can be found in most of North America. They are mostly red-orange in color, but also have patches of white and black. The red fox has a bushy tail and pointed ears. These foxes are omnivores and are mostly active at night. The red fox will eat berries, birds, and small mammals. They will even store food when they are too full to eat.

The flowering dogwood (*Cornus florida*) is a tree in the forest ***understory*** that provides food for many animals, including deer and foxes. It reminds us of the cross of Jesus because it has a flower shaped like a cross. At the tip of each petal is a dent that looks like it was made by a nail. The "nail dents" are stained with a red color, like Jesus' blood. In the center of each flower is a green cluster that reminds us of Jesus' crown of thorns.

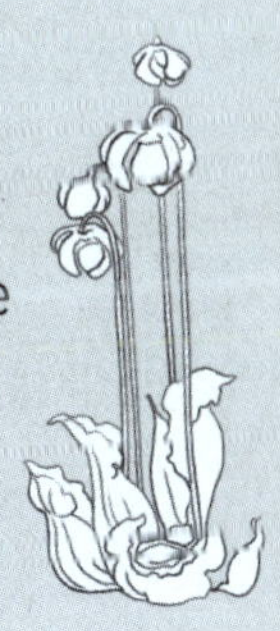

Blessed Frederic Janssoone

Frederic Janssoone was born in 1838. He became a Franciscan priest in France, but he ended up in Canada due to some interesting circumstances. Frederic had been sent to the Holy Land, where Franciscans take care of the holy places, including the tomb of Jesus. He made a trip back to France to raise money to take care of these shrines, but he did not succeed. A priest from Canada invited him to raise money in Canada, and Father Frederic ended up staying in Canada, where everyone loved to hear him preach. He set up an outdoor Stations of the Cross to give people an opportunity to pray the way people were doing in Jerusalem. (See page 40 for making your own outdoor Stations of the Cross.)

Reptiles and Amphibians of the Temperate Deciduous Forest

Reptiles are known for their ability to move about on the forest floor and in the trees very quietly. Reptiles include snakes, turtles, and lizards. There are also many kinds of amphibians in this forest biome, such as frogs, toads, newts, and salamanders. These amphibians live on trees and under fallen logs, and like to eat insects and other small forest animals. They also eat plants. The temperate deciduous forest is a great place for amphibians, because it contains moisture from the trees and constant shade, something that amphibians need.

Eastern box turtle (*Terrapene carolina carolina*) The eastern box turtle is a land turtle that lives as far north as Maine, as far south as Florida, and as far west as Texas! It is slow moving and can be different hues of orange and brown. These turtles are omnivores: they will eat a variety of plants and even earthworms! Box turtles need our protection. They are declining because their forest habitat is being destroyed, and also because people take them out of the forest to be pets. When box turtles are removed from their wild homes, they usually die.

NATURE JOURNAL IDEA

Write a letter for your community newspaper encouraging people to leave wild animals in the wild.

Gray tree frog (*Dryophytes versicolor*) The gray tree frog is found in many parts of the United States and southeastern Canada. These beautiful frogs live in the treetops and only come down when it is time to lay eggs. The gray tree frog is not always gray. It can change color like a chameleon in order to hide from predators. Depending on where it sits, this tree frog can be gray or green, or one of the many tones in between!

PRAYER

Dear Lord, we thank you for these beautiful and fruitful forests that you have provided for us. We thank you for the trees and the life-giving oxygen they provide, and we thank you for the many creatures of the forest, our little brothers and sisters that live there. We ask that you guide us as we work to be good stewards of these precious resources and help us to work together to care for them so that they may live on into the future. Amen.

ACTIVITY

Flash Like a Firefly!

Fireflies are amazing insects that live in and around forests. The males use special chemicals inside their bodies to attract mates by lighting up. This ability to flash is called bioluminescence. The flashing also warns predators that these special chemicals taste bad. Different species of fireflies use different flash patterns. For example, some flash once every second or every two seconds; others flash a couple times in a row every few seconds.

Materials: Nature Journal, pencil, flashlight, internet source (optional)

Instructions: Use some of the firefly flash patterns described above, or research different firefly flash patterns and record your findings. You can even imagine your own species of firefly and give it its own flash patterns. Go outside at night or simply into a dark place and use a flashlight to create your own firefly flashes. You can have another young scientist use your research to guess what species you are pretending to be!

ACTIVITY

Spot the Scat

Did you know that scientists can learn a lot about animals through their scat? (Scat is scientists' name for poop.)

Materials: Natural Journal, pencil, play dough (optional)

Instructions: Go on a nature walk in the forest and look for any scat on the ground. Deer and rabbit scat are both common in the deciduous forest biome. They are both pill shaped, but deer scat is larger and shinier. Record what you find in your nature journal. If you can't hit the trails, research different kinds of scat near you. Try making models of the scat with play dough or any other material on hand. Teach and quiz another scientist using your models!

Chapter 8

Our Home in the Coniferous Forest

Coniferous forests have plant life composed primarily of needle-leaved or scale-leaved evergreen trees with cones. These evergreens are also called ***conifers***. Coniferous forests are found in areas that have long winters and moderate to high amounts of snow and rain.

In the coniferous forest, the soil may be acidic. It does not contain as many nutrients as a deciduous forest. Therefore, the different kinds of plants that grow here are adapted to these conditions.

Many of the psalms in the Bible speak of forests and the animals that live there. The Bible mentions many times how these creatures glorify God by their existence.

> Let the heavens be glad, and let the earth rejoice;
> let the sea roar and all that fills it;
> let the field exult and everything in it.
> Then shall all the trees of the forest sing for joy
> before the Lord, for he is coming . . . (Psalm 96:11–13).

> "For every wild animal of the forest is mine,
> the cattle on a thousand hills.
> I know all the birds of the air,
> and all that moves in the field is mine" (Psalm 50:9–11).

✝ *Saint John Gualberto*

Saint John Gualberto lived in Italy in the eleventh century. He had joined a monastery, but he wanted to live a more strict life. He visited some hermits but thought it would be better to live in community with other monks. So he started a new monastery at Vallombrosa, which means "shady valley." He and his brother monks planted trees (especially the conifers called firs) instead of a regular garden. He is a patron saint of foresters, park rangers, and parks.

NATURE JOURNAL IDEA

A mature coniferous forest usually has fewer layers than a temperate deciduous forest. Often there are just a canopy and an undergrowth layer. In addition to the poor soil in many coniferous forests, conifers create a lot of shade, have deep roots, and compete for water and nutrients, so many plants can't survive under them. Go outside and draw or record the kinds of plants you see living under the trees near you. If possible, compare plants living under a clump of coniferous trees with the plants living in a patch of deciduous woods.

Plants of the Coniferous Forest

In the coniferous forest, you will find many types of trees, shrubs, and herbs (wildflowers, ferns, and grasses). Trees in the forest grow tall and are adapted to absorb sunlight from up high and have thick canopies. Some plants can't get nutrients from the soil here, so they get what they need in a different way—by becoming carnivorous!

White spruce (*Picea glauca*) The white spruce is one of the most widespread coniferous trees in North America, with a range across the eastern United States and Canada. It is one of the most popular Christmas tree choices. The white spruce has pointy, but not sharp, needles. These spruces can grow

Poor logging practices can be a threat to coniferous forests. It is important that when people harvest trees for their wood, they take care to manage the area so habitats will not be destroyed.

fifty to one hundred feet tall and live for two hundred and fifty to three hundred years.

In the coniferous forest, you will also find many kinds of shrubs. These plants are not as tall as trees and can survive in the shade underneath the branches of trees. Shrubs also produce berries that are important food sources for animals.

Common snowberry (*Symphoricarpos albus*) The common snowberry shrub is a unique plant that has bright white berries. This shrub can be found all over the United States and Canada. In the west, it is eaten by many animals, even the grizzly bear! Bears eat the berries, and small rodents burrow under its branches. This plant is the host plant of a very special insect called the snowberry clearwing moth, a moth that comes out during the day and looks like a hummingbird as it sips nectar from the flowers. This moth lays eggs on the shrub, and its caterpillars eat the leaves.

Purple pitcher plant (*Sarracenia purpurea*) This plant is carnivorous. It eats meat! It is bright purple, and it lures insects into its hollow, pitcher-like leaves. Once the insect goes in, the plant closes and eats the insect!

Native Americans have used the snowberry plant to make soap, but these berries are not for eating. They can give you a stomachache. Make sure never to eat any berries unless an expert has identified them as safe.

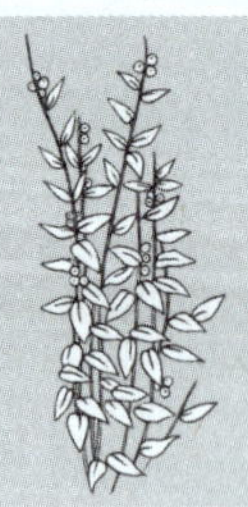

Our Lady of Good Help

In 1859, in the woods near Champion, Wisconsin, a young woman named Adele Brise was walking on a trail. She saw a vision of a woman standing in light, between two trees: a maple and a hemlock. This happened three times. The third time, the lady told Adele, "I am the Queen of Heaven." She asked Adele to pray for the conversion of sinners and to teach children about God. Adele was worried because she did not feel capable of doing this, but Mary said, "Go and fear nothing. I will help you." For the rest of her life, Adele taught children the Gospel. Now, you can visit the very place Adele saw our Lady, Mary, at the Shrine of Our Lady of Good Help in Wisconsin.

NATURE JOURNAL IDEA

What might it be like to walk along outside and suddenly see Mary, the Mother of Jesus, standing in front of you? Write about what you think it would be like and what you would do.

Animals of the Coniferous Forest

The different types of animals that live in the coniferous forest are adapted to survive in shaded environments. They are able to survive the cold that comes with the snows of winter.

When a person sees a vision of Mary, it is called an apparition. The Church carefully investigates when people claim to have seen Mary. Even when apparitions have been officially approved, like this one called Our Lady of Good Help, the Church does not require Catholics to believe in apparitions. You can go online to find the stories of Marian apparitions throughout history.

Arthropods of the Coniferous Forest

The coniferous forest is home to many insects, especially in the summer. Bark beetles and wood boring beetles feed on the many trees.

Taiga alpine butterfly (*Erebia mancinus*) Even the coniferous forest has butterflies! The taiga alpine is a beautiful dark butterfly with orange spots. Its caterpillar feeds on grasses, and it lives in bogs.

Jumping spiders (*Metaphidippus* spp.) There are many species of jumping spiders, several of which live in coniferous forests. They are important parts of the ecosystem because they eat many kinds of insects that harm trees. They also eat the eggs of those insects. These spiders were named *jumping* because most of them do not use webs to trap their prey. Instead, they hunt for their prey and pounce on them.

Birds of the Coniferous Forest

Birds of the coniferous forest are adapted to find food that comes from the many coniferous trees that live there. These birds eat seeds from the pine and fir cones as well as insects that live inside the trees. To nest or take shelter from storms, they find cavities, or holes, in trees.

If you thought about forest birds, you probably thought of owls! Forest owls are brown or grey in color to blend in with the branches. The great grey owl is the largest owl in the world by length, with a grey body and large yellow eyes. It hunts small rodents called voles, sometimes breaking through the snow to catch them. It lives in the western coniferous forests and has a deep hoot for a call. You can identify owls at night by learning their songs and calls.

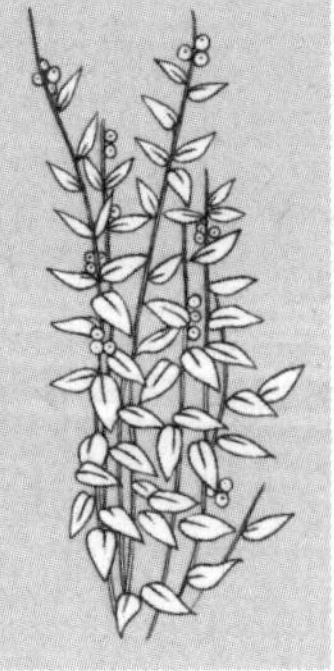

Black-capped chickadee (*Poecile atricapillus*) The black-capped chickadee is a small black and white songbird with what looks like a black mask on its face. Black-capped chickadees live in the forests of the north and midwestern United States and are widespread in Canada. They are named for the unique sound they make when calling to one another: *chickadee dee dee dee*! In the winter, chickadees call out to other birds when they find a good food source. This is why other species of birds, such as nuthatches, can be found in the same flock as chickadees during the winter. Chickadees like to feast on small insects that live in the bark of trees.

Red crossbill (*Loxia curvirostra*) The red crossbill is a small bird in the finch family. It gets its name from its red body color, which is brighter on its rear end. Its wings are brown. Its beak, also called a bill, is not crossed at first, but as a young bird grows its beak gets twisted when removing seeds from cones. This position eventually becomes permanent, so the adult bird has a crossed bill. These little birds feed on conifer seeds and are widespread in the coniferous forests of North America.

If you have a forest habitat in your backyard, you might be able to attract chickadees by providing a birdhouse that has a small entrance hole. Check online to see what size of house and hole you will need. There are different species of chickadees in different parts of North America. On the west coast, the mountain chickadee makes its home. The Carolina chickadee can be found in the southern U.S., and up into the northeast as well.

Mammals of the Coniferous Forest

Mammals of the forest are adapted to eat the plants and small animals that live there. In the coniferous forest, there are larger animals like bears, deer, moose, and wolves. There are also many smaller animals like foxes, chipmunks, and mice. Some small animals are able to climb trees. Each mammal has its own niche that it fills in the forest ecosystem.

Brown bear (*Ursus arctos*) Bears are incredible organisms. They are one of the largest animals of the forest, and a primary predator. They are omnivores, meaning they eat both meat and plants. Some favorite foods of bears are berries and fish. Brown bears ***hibernate***, meaning that when the weather gets cold they eat large amounts of food and then sleep for the whole winter, until the weather is warm again. A subspecies of brown bear, the grizzly, is a large bear with brown fur that has silvery tips, giving it the name *grizzly*. These bears live in the forests and mountain regions of the western United States and Canada. Other brown bears live along the coast.

Bears will usually stay away if they hear you coming from far away. When hiking in areas that have bears, always walk in groups, avoid walking at dawn and dusk when bears are most active, wear bells on your walking stick and gear, and talk loudly. Many hikers shout, "Hey bear!" while hiking. An adult can also bring bear spray, a peppery substance to spray if you do find yourself face to face with a bear. Remember to NEVER feed bears, because this can attract them to people. It is important to be good stewards and protect forests so that bears may live in peace in their home!

Gray wolf (*Canis lupus*) The gray wolf is the largest wild member of the dog family. Gray wolves are canines with long bushy tails that are often black-tipped. They look somewhat like large German shepherds, but they vary in size depending on where they live. Wolves in the north are usually larger than those in the south. Wolves are carnivores—they prefer to eat large, hoofed mammals, such as deer, elk, bison, and moose. They also hunt smaller mammals, such as beavers, hares, and other rodents.

Saint John Bosco

Saint John Bosco was a priest who worked to help poor and homeless boys in Italy in the nineteenth century. He opened an oratory, which was a home for the boys to live in. At the time, there were people who were against John Bosco and his work, and against the Catholic Church. When John went out at night, his life was in danger. One evening when he was coming home late and alone, a huge, gray dog that looked almost like a wolf came up to him. At first John was afraid of it, but the dog was friendly and walked home with him. Over the years, the dog showed up many times to be with John when he traveled at night. A few times, the dog saved his life when someone tried to attack him!

Reptiles and Amphibians of the Coniferous Forest

Fewer species of reptiles and amphibians exist in the coniferous forest, especially in the north. The cold temperatures make it harder for them to survive because their body temperatures get very low. Reptiles and amphibians that do live in these forests live on trees and under fallen logs. They eat insects and other forest animals and plants.

Blue spotted salamander (*Ambystoma laterale*) The blue spotted salamander is one species of amphibians found in the coniferous forest. It is known for its dark body with blue and white flecks on its skin. The salamander likes to live in ***vernal pools***, small pools that fill with water after a rain. Vernal pools are very important habitats to protect!

Northern alligator lizard (*Elgaria coerulea*) Northern alligator lizards are medium sized reptiles that resemble alligators because of their short legs and long tails. Like most lizards, they can drop their tails to throw off predators. This reptile's tail will even move when it is no longer attached to the body! Over time the tail of a healthy lizard will grow back. Northern alligator lizards are secretive and hard to find. They like to live in rocky areas of the forest.

PRAYER

Here is one way to use a psalm for prayer: Sit in a quiet place and begin with the Sign of the Cross, then read the psalm slowly and thoughtfully. What word or phrase seems meaningful to you? Think about that word or phrase and talk to God about it. End your prayer with the Sign of the Cross.

> The trees of the Lord are watered abundantly,
> the cedars of Lebanon that he planted.
> In them the birds build their nests;
> the stork has its home in the fir trees. . . .

You have made the moon to mark the seasons;
the sun knows its time for setting.
You make darkness, and it is night,
when all the animals of the forest come creeping out. . . .
When the sun rises, they withdraw
and lie down in their dens.
People go out to their work
and to their labor until the evening.

— Psalm 104:16–23

Reuse Your Christmas Tree

Christmas trees are coniferous trees! Buying a live Christmas tree that you can plant afterward, rather than a cut tree, is actually better for the environment. (In some areas, you can even rent a potted tree for Christmas.) Legend says that Saint Francis wanted all of creation to participate in Christmas, and that no one should be excluded, not even the birds. He asked people to scatter grain in the streets so that the birds would not go hungry and could celebrate too!

If your family chooses to buy a live tree, you can repurpose it after Christmas by placing it in your yard and decorating it with bird food ornaments. Of course, you could decorate a tree with these bird-friendly ornaments any time of year.

Materials: Christmas tree with the ornaments removed (or any live evergreen tree in your yard), birdseed, plate or pan, pinecones, peanut butter, two oranges cut into slices, a few twigs, string.

Instructions: Place your used Christmas tree up against a fence or another tree. Pour the birdseed onto a flat plate or pan. Use twigs to spread the pinecones with peanut butter, then dip them in birdseed. Use string to hang the orange slices and your pinecone ornaments on the tree. Then watch birds and animals enjoy a winter treat!

Conifer Quest

Materials: Nature Journal, pencil

Instructions: Go outside and look at the different types of leaves the conifers have. Compare and contrast the structures. Are they flattened? Are they needle-like? How many needles are in each cluster? If there aren't any conifers near you, compare the leaves of the trees in your area to the conifer leaves in this book. In your journal record or draw what you see.

Chapter 9

Our Home in the Temperate Rainforest

When you think of a rainforest, you probably think of a hot, tropical environment. Believe it or not, a rainforest can exist in a temperate climate too! ***Rainforests*** are thick forests that grow in wet areas of the world. In fact, temperate rainforests exist in North America—in Alaska, parts of Canada, in the Pacific Northwestern states of Washington, Oregon, and California, and even in the Appalachian Mountains of the Southeastern states.

A ***temperate rainforest*** is a forest with a moderate climate that experiences a lot of rainfall—over twelve feet of rain in one year! On the west coast, this rain happens in winter. In the summer, the forest receives its moisture from fog, especially near the ocean.

Many of the temperate rainforests of North America occur in the mountains. As Catholics, we honor a special person who loved the mountains too!

✝ *Saint Pier Giorgio Frassati*

Pier Giorgio lived in Italy in the 1900s and loved to climb mountains. He once wrote, "Every day that passes I fall more and more in love with the mountains; if it weren't for my studies, I would spend entire days up in the pure mountain air, contemplating the greatness of the Creator."[13] Once on the back of a photo, he wrote the words *Verso l'alto,* which means, *upward* in Italian. By this he meant both upward to the top of the mountain, and upward to heaven. Pier Giorgio cared very much for the poor and during his life did many good works to help them.

Plants of the Temperate Rainforest

Temperate rainforests are mostly made of coniferous trees with broadleaf shrubs and other types of shrubs in the understory. All the moisture present in the forest allows for many plant species to grow, especially ***epiphytes***. Epiphyte is a word used to describe plants that grow on the surface of other plants, usually trees. Examples of epiphytes are mosses, ferns, algae, and lichens. Epiphytes have roots, but these roots can pull moisture from the air, from bodies of water in marine environments, or from the surface of the host tree. The moisture in the forest also allows for many species of fungi to grow. Some species may even be undiscovered!

✝ *Saint Bernard of Clairvaux*

This holy man was an abbot in France in the twelfth century. He was a writer and a very good preacher. He traveled a lot to preach, but he most loved to stay in the abbey. He and his monks had built the abbey in an isolated area to be able to spend time in prayer. He once wrote to advise a man to also become a monk: "You will find more lessons in the woods than in books. Trees and stones will teach you what you cannot learn from masters."[14] Saint Bernard is a Doctor of the Church, and his writings help many people today.

Coast redwood (*Sequoia sempervirens*) The coast redwood, also known as the California redwood or giant redwood, is a species of tree that grows in the temperate rainforest. It lives in areas that are very wet and have lots of fog. These amazing trees can live for up to two thousand years and grow to more than three hundred feet tall! Their branches provide shelter for many species, such as the threatened northern spotted owl (*Strix occidentalis caurina*). Indigenous people, such as the Yurok, have a special relationship with the redwood. They use the redwood for many different things, and it has great spiritual importance for them. Some Indigenous groups still live in the redwood forests today.

Western hemlock (*Tsuga heterophylla*) Western hemlocks like shade. They produce small cones and have relationships with fungi, which allows their seedlings to grow on rotting logs. In the spring, branches from this tree are used by Alaska Natives to gather herring eggs from the rivers, as they have traditionally done for many years!

Salmonberry (*Rubus spectabilis*) Salmonberry is a shrub of the Pacific Northwest, growing in temperate rainforests. The berry was eaten by Indigenous peoples, often together with salmon as a part of the meal. Salmonberries are a very important food source in the forest—even banana slugs eat them!

NATURE JOURNAL IDEA

Mosses are flowerless plants without true roots. They are found in every biome and even though they thrive with moisture and shade, certain mosses are also common in the desert. The temperate rainforest is home to many kinds of moss. Many mosses look like green mats, but they can also be different colors. They can be found on trees, rocks, buildings, soils, other plants, and even on animals! Go outside with your nature journal and magnifying glass (optional) and draw or record the kinds of mosses around you and what they are growing on.

In temperate rainforests, fallen logs serve as a place for seedlings to grow. When this happens, these dead trees are called ***nurse logs***.

Animals of the Temperate Rainforest

Animals of the temperate rainforest are adapted to a lot of rainfall, as well as a cool temperature. Many kinds of insects live in the temperate rainforest: different kinds of bees, butterflies, ants, and more. The moist environment gives insects and other arthropods like spiders many places to hide and lots of food to eat.

Arthropods of the Temperate Rainforest

Yellow spotted millipede (*Harpaphe haydeniana*) The yellow spotted millipede is common in the temperate rainforests of the west coasts. When these arthropods are mature, they have long black bodies with yellow spots that serve as a warning to predators. They are also known as the cyanide millipede, because they release cyanide, a toxic substance. The amount of cyanide isn't dangerous to humans. The yellow spotted millipede is a type of consumer called a ***decomposer***, which breaks down, or decomposes, food. Decomposers play an important role in cycling nutrients.

Conifer lady beetle (*Scymnus coniferarum*) The conifer lady beetle is found in the temperate rainforests on the west coasts of Canada and the United States. They are small carnivores. They play an important role in the ecosystem because they eat other arthropods that damage trees like the hemlock.

Mammals of the Temperate Rainforest

Various mammals live in the temperate rainforest, and they all have an impact on the habitat they live in. There are hooved animals like the moose and Roosevelt elk, predators like the mountain lion, and smaller mammals as well. The large trees and moisture are important to these mammals as shelter and food. As in other biomes, mammals of the temperate rain forest help plants by returning nutrients to the soil in their scat!

Mountain lion (*Puma concolor*) Mountain lions in the temperate rainforest can camouflage easily because of their brown and tan color. They hunt by stalking their prey, usually elk and black-tailed deer.

Roosevelt elk (*Cervus canadensis roosevelti*) The roosevelt elk is a subspecies of the North American elk and is the largest elk in body size in North America. One reason that President Theodore Roosevelt created the Mount Olympus National Monument was to protect the elk in that area. This type of elk is an ***indicator species***. This means that the health of the Roosevelt elk population tells us a lot about the ecosystem as a whole. Roosevelt elk like to eat shrubs, grasses, and even lichens!

Saint Martin de Porres

Saint Martin was born in Peru in 1579. His father was a nobleman from Spain and his mother was a freed slave from Panama. Martin learned the trade of a barber—which at that time included not just cutting hair, but also making herbal medicines, treating sickness,

Saint Thérèse of Lisieux said, "If all flowers wanted to be roses, nature would lose her springtime beauty, and the fields would no longer be decked out with little wild flowers."[15] This quote means we should appreciate not only the diversity of plants and animals, but also the diversity of people! We are all different with our own gifts to offer.

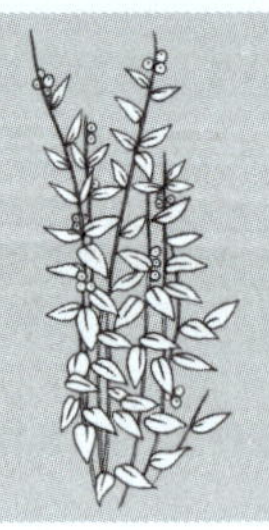

and performing surgery. Martin continued this work after entering the Dominican order. The religious brothers all depended on his care. In addition to caring for people, Martin treated injured and sick animals, especially dogs. He even took care of the mice that were infesting the monastery. Instead of putting out poison to get rid of them, he asked them to stay in the garden, and he brought food out to them.

Birds of the Temperate Rainforest

Bald eagle (*Haliaeetus leucocephalus*) Bald eagles are well-known raptors (birds of prey) that are found in most of North America. These large birds chiefly eat fish and are found near water. They like to nest in old trees, which is one reason why it is important to keep forests intact. The United States has chosen the bald eagle as its national symbol. Eagles are mentioned in Scripture many times as a symbol of courage and faith.. This example is from the book of the prophet Isaiah:

> ". . . but those who wait for the Lord shall renew their strength;
>   they shall mount up with wings like eagles;
> they shall run and not be weary;
>   they shall walk and not faint" (Isaiah 40:31).

The eagle also is a symbol of the evangelist (Gospel writer) Saint John.

Steller's jay (*Cyanocitta stelleri*) The Stellar's jay lives in the temperate rainforest and other forest biomes. It looks much like the blue jay but has a completely black head. Steller's jays are omnivores. They mostly feast on acorns and nuts, but can also eat rodents and even small reptiles. Jays are part of the corvid family, so they are related to crows. This family of birds is well known for being smart!

Northern spotted owl (*Strix occidentalis caurina*) The northern spotted owl is a rare species of owl that lives in the temperate rainforest of the Pacific Northwest. This owl is medium sized and brown with spots. It thrives in areas where there are old trees with lots of dead snags and wood. There are fewer spotted owls in North America than there once were, because forests are being destroyed by logging. This has made the spotted owl a threatened species.

NATURE JOURNAL IDEA

Did you know that fog is a kind of cloud that touches the ground? The temperate rainforest has less rain than a tropical rainforest, but it also receives a lot of moisture from fog. Take your nature journal outside and observe the kinds of clouds near you throughout the day. Draw or record your observations. Did any particular shapes of clouds lead to rain or another kind of precipitation? What time of day or night did this happen? If you were to observe the sky over the course of a few days, do you think there would be a pattern? Try it out!

Reptiles and Amphibians of the Temperate Rainforest

The temperate rainforest is home to many amphibians and several reptile species. The rain and fog allow for lots of wet wood and pools that amphibians like to live in.

Pacific giant salamander (*Dicamptodon ensatus*) The pacific giant salamander is a unique amphibian found only in northwestern temperate rainforests. These salamanders can grow to be thirteen inches long! The salamander starts its life in the water, then spends its adult life under fallen logs and rocks both in and out of the water. It eats smaller salamanders and fish.

Pacific tree frog (*Pseudacris regilla*) The pacific tree frog is a small amphibian that uses camouflage to protect itself from predators. It can change its color depending on the temperature and humidity of the air around it. It has a stripe that runs from its nostrils to its shoulder. It is also called the pacific chorus frog because of its high pitched "singing."

PRAYER

Joseph Chiwatenwha was a Native American from the Wyandot tribe (also called the Huron tribe) who became Catholic. He had a deep love for God and taught many people about the Catholic faith. He was a great help to the Jesuit missionaries in finding ways to explain the Gospel stories so that his people would understand them. Here is part of a prayer he wrote:

> "O God, at last I start to understand you. You made the Earth, which we live in. You made the sky, which we see above us. You made us, we who are called people. Now you let me start to know who you really are. I know how to make a canoe, and how to enjoy it. I know how to build a cabin and how to live in it. But you . . . you made us,

In the temperate rainforest of the southeastern United States, there are over thirty species of salamanders, some found nowhere else in the world! You can visit parts of the Appalachian temperate rainforest in the Cherokee National Forest and Great Smoky National Park.

and you live in us. The things we make last for a few seasons. We only use the canoes we create for a short time. We only live in the houses we build for a few years. But your love for us will endure so long that we cannot count the time. You will comfort us forever. Amen."[16]

Create a Tree of Life

The tree of life is mentioned in the Old Testament as a symbol of God's life-giving power. We consider Christ's cross as our Tree of Life because Christ brought life to us through his death on the cross. We can reflect on this idea by creating a cross from a real tree!

Materials: Nature Journal, pencil, clear packing tape, thick piece of paper or cardboard, two sticks (one longer and one shorter), wildflowers and leaves, heavy books, newspaper or other scrap paper

Instructions: Venture into your yard or a park and while you explore, collect the sticks, leaves, and wildflowers that you will need. Be sure to only pick common flowers, so the rare wildflowers can have the best chance to grow! When you get home, arrange your sticks into a cross and tape them down to the cardboard. Press your flowers and leaves by putting them between two sheets of paper (newspaper or parchment paper if you have it). Then place them inside a heavy book. You can check on the flowers every day to see if they are dry and flattened. Some plants take longer to dry than others. Record your observations in your journal. Afterward you can carefully take the flowers out. They will be very thin, so work slowly. You can now use them to decorate the cross you made!

ACTIVITY

Make and Pray a Natural Rosary

You can create a living rosary in your backyard! See page 179 for more about the rosary and how to pray it.

Materials: Fifty small natural items (one for each Hail Mary), five medium sized items (for the Our Fathers), and two sticks to make a cross.

Instructions: Search along the ground for small, medium, and large items like nuts, seeds, and flowers. (You could also use stones, although they are not living.) Arrange your items on the ground in the shape of a rosary and gather your family to pray!

Did you know that some nuns and sisters have been making rosary beads from real rose petals for centuries? To create the beads, they dry real rose petals, then make them into a paste and shape them into beads.

Chapter 10

Our Home in the Tropical Rainforest

A ***tropical rainforest*** is a dense forest with tall trees that receives more than eighty inches of rain each year. That is a lot of rain! Tropical rainforests are found near the Equator, an imaginary circle around the middle of the Earth that divides the northern and southern hemispheres.

Tropical rainforests are dominated by broad-leaved trees that form a dense canopy (layer of plant leaves). About half of the world's plant and animal species live in rainforests—with new species yet to be discovered!

Most rainforests receive rain year-round, but some rainforests have a dry season. In the United States, tropical rainforests are found in Puerto Rico and Hawaii. In addition to having tropical rainforests, Hawaii and Puerto Rico are also unique because they are islands. Islands are special because they allow plants and animals to evolve isolated from other organisms on the mainland. Therefore, on these islands there are species found nowhere else in the world! Species found in only one place are called ***endemic*** species. However, being located on islands, the forests of Hawaii and Puerto Rico have fewer species of land mammals and reptiles than places like the Amazon rainforest.

When you think of a tropical forest, you probably first think of a palm tree. Many species of palm trees grow in the tropics. They are also found in temperate areas and in the desert or near the seashore when there is groundwater present.

Palm trees are mentioned often in Scripture! Psalm 92:12 says, "The righteous shall flourish like a palm tree. He shall grow like a cedar in

Aloha! Native Hawaiian people have a rich culture and beautiful language. Ancient Hawaiians knew how to use many native Hawaiian plants like the hibiscus, which they used for dye and for building fishing nets. Native Hawaiian plants are still a large part of Hawaiian culture and traditions today.

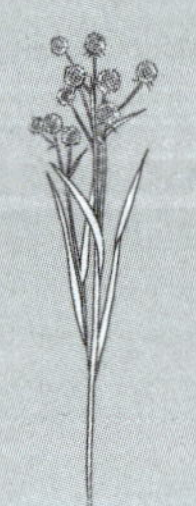

Lebanon." In the New Testament, when Jesus entered the temple in Jerusalem, his disciples took palm branches and laid them at his feet. Palms are a symbol of victory.

✝ *Sister Dorothy Stang*

Sister Dorothy was a member of the congregation of the Sisters of Notre Dame de Namur. She was born in the United States and was also a citizen of Brazil. Sister Dorothy spent much of her life in the Amazon Basin, trying to prevent the destruction of the Amazon rainforest and working for the well-being of the poor people living there. A new species of screech owl is even named after her: *Megascops stangiae*. Sister Dorothy said, "STOP! Give yourself space to smell the flowers and marvel at nature."[17] You can read more about Sister Dorothy Stang on the website of the Sisters of Notre Dame de Namur.

Plants of the Tropical Rainforest

Like temperate rainforests, tropical rainforests have many diverse species of plants. Trees have evergreen leaves, such as the many species of palm trees. ***Epiphytes*** also grow in tropical rainforests. Epiphytes are plants that grow on other trees. Orchids are one type of epiphyte in North American tropical forests. There are many beautiful and unique species of orchids in the tropical rainforest! Plants in these forests come in many colors, shapes, and sizes.

Sierra palm tree (*Prestoea montana*) The Sierra palm is a tree native to Puerto Rico and other Caribbean islands. It has large roots that stick out, helping it to adapt to soil conditions. This palm tree's fruit is the favorite food of the Puerto Rican parrot.

Jewel orchid (*Anoectochilus sandvicensis*) The jewel orchid is the most common of the three native species of orchid found in Hawaii. All three species are rare. It is called a jewel orchid because of its attractive flowers and leaves.

NATURE JOURNAL IDEA

The biodiversity of the tropical rainforest makes it full of sounds, sights and smells. Go outside with your nature journal, close your eyes for a few minutes, and then open them and record everything you heard. Now, close your eyes again for a few minutes and then open them and record everything you smelled. Finally, look around and record what you see. Was there anything there that you didn't notice when you first arrived?

Animals of the Tropical Rainforest

Animals in the tropical rainforest are unique and depend on the abundance of water and plants that are found there. Animals in this biome have many adaptations, such as camouflage to hide among their surroundings. Also, in the tropical rainforest animals tend to be smaller so they can

The Taino people are Indigenous peoples of the Caribbean, including Puerto Rico. Ancient Taino relied on farming, fishing, and a close relationship with nature to survive. Many ancient Taino traditions continue today. Also, you probably would recognize some Taino words. English words like *hammock*, *barbecue*, *hurricane*, *canoe*, and *iguana* were derived from Taino words.

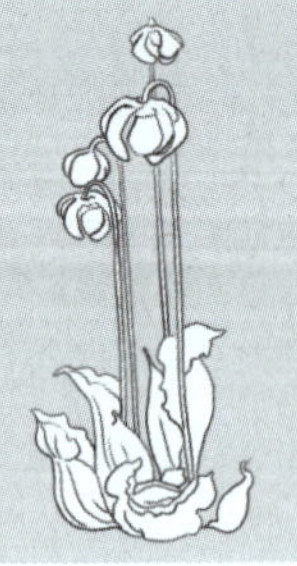

more easily avoid predators in dense vegetation. Rainforest animals can even mimic one another!

Arthropods of the Tropical Rainforest

All tropical rainforests are known for their diversity of arthropods, but Hawaii has over five thousand endemic insects! Puerto Rico has eighteen endemic insect species.

Happy-face spider (*Theridion grallator*) The happy-face spider is found on only a few islands of Hawaii. The spider looks like it has a happy face painted on its back. The face may help stop birds and other animals from eating them.

Masked bees (*Hylaeus* spp.) Masked bees are the only family of bees considered native to the Hawaiian Islands, and there are many species of them—more than anywhere else in the United States! They get their name from a little white or yellow patch between their eyes that makes them look like they're wearing masks.

Koa butterfly (*Udara Blackburnii*) The koa butterfly has a blue color on the outside of its wings and green on the inside. It is found only in Hawaii. They like to eat the leaves of the koa tree, another native plant.

Birds of the Tropical Rainforest

Fruits, nuts, and seeds make up the food of many Hawaiian and Puerto Rican birds. Because they live on islands, many kinds of birds that have evolved here are specialized. Like the other kinds of animals in the tropical rainforest, birds in this type of forest are extremely colorful with unique adaptations.

Hawaiian honeycreeper (*Drepanidinae* spp.) Honeycreepers are a group of fifty related birds that evolved in the forests of the Hawaiian Islands. It is theorized that all the honeycreepers evolved from one flock of rose finches that arrived at the islands around seven million years ago. Their beaks are specially shaped to eat nectar from flowers. The 'i'iwi (pronounced *ee-EE-vee*) or scarlet honeycreeper (*Drepanis coccinea*) is a common honeycreeper of the tropical rainforest.

Puerto Rican parrot (*Amazona vittata*) This parrot is one of the ten rarest birds in the world and is only found on the Island of Puerto Rico. The parrot is green with a red forehead and white rings around the eyes. These parrots used to number in the hundreds of thousands. Today, there are only about 350 Puerto Rican parrots remaining in the wild. Conservationists are working to save the species.

Blessed María Agustina Rivas Lopez

Blessed María Agustina was a religious sister in Peru. The country of Peru has several biomes, including deserts, grasslands, and tropical forests. Much of the country is mountainous. María Agustina was born in the mountainous region, and then worked as a sister in the desert area, till near the end of her life, when she went to work in the tropical forest region, particularly with poor Indigenous women. She knew that she was living in a dangerous area, but she remained there to help the people. Blessed María Augstina was killed by terrorists in 1990.

Mammals of the Tropical Rainforest

Hawaii and Puerto Rico are unique because they are islands. In these tropical island ecosystems, only one type of living land mammal is truly native: the bat. Hawaii has one bat species, while Puerto Rico has eighteen. All other land mammals have been introduced from other places. Sometimes these land mammals are ***invasive,*** and conservationists must try to remove them from the islands.

Hawaiian hoary bat (*Lasirus cinereus semotus*) The Hawaiian hoary bat is the only land mammal that is native to Hawaii. Its fur is brown and gray, with white tips to the hairs that give the bat a frosted or "hoarfrost" look. The bats roost in trees, hidden in the ***foliage*** (leaves), and hunt for food, such as insects, by flying over open areas.

Greater bulldog bat (*Noctilio leporinus*) The greater bulldog bat is one of the eighteen native bat species in Puerto Rico. These are the only bats in Puerto Rico that eat fish, but they will also eat insects if they need to. This bat gets its name from the folded skin under its nostrils, giving it the appearance of a bulldog.

Gastropods

Gastropods are a group of invertebrate animals that includes snails and slugs. Though most are also found in other biomes, there are more than 750 species of snails in the tropical forests of the Hawaiian Islands. Millions of years ago, these snails most likely arrived in the islands by sticking onto the feathers of birds or floating tree trunks. Many species of snails are becoming very rare.

Kāhuli tree snail (*Achatinella* spp.) These native tree snails can only be found on one island, Oahu. With their shiny, earth-tone shells, they adorn native trees and look like Christmas tree decorations. These snails help keep trees healthy by eating fungus. One of their biggest predators is an invasive species, the rosy wolf snail.

Reptiles and Amphibians of the Tropical Rainforest

Because they are islands, Hawaii and Puerto Rico do not have as many native species of reptiles or amphibians as do other tropical rainforests. In fact, there are no native frogs or toads present in Hawaii. Puerto Rico does have native frogs and snakes and one native toad species.

Puerto Rican coqui frog (*Eleutherodactylus coqui*) In Puerto Rico, the coqui frog is a cultural symbol. The coqui frog lives in trees in the tropical forest. It has a loud voice commonly heard at night!

Puerto Rican racer (*Borikenophis portoricensis*) The Puerto Rican racer is the largest snake in Puerto Rico, yet it is only three feet long. When scared it will stand up on its belly and look almost like a cobra! It loves to eat coqui frogs in the forest.

Islands often have problems with invasive species, because invasive species cause damage to ***habitats***. It is important to manage invasive species for the health of ecosystems. Invasive species live in every biome.

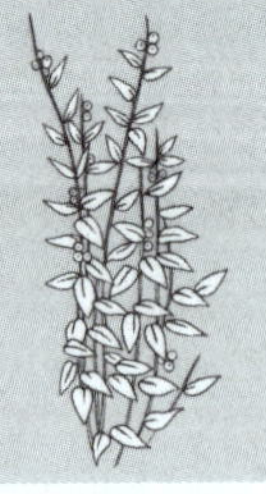

Saint Joseph Vaz

Saint Joseph Vaz was born in India in the mid-seventeenth century. After being ordained a priest, he went to carry out his ministry on the nearby island of Sri Lanka, which has several biomes, including tropical rainforests. The Dutch had taken over the island and had sent away all the Catholic priests, so Joseph had to travel around in disguise. He celebrated Mass with the Catholics whenever and wherever he could. As he dressed as a farm worker or beggar and hid in the forests, Joseph would have seen many beautiful plants and animals. Currently, there are 120 known species of amphibians on Sri Lanka, and 109 of them are endemic.

NATURE JOURNAL IDEA

We say we pray "in communion" with all the saints. That means that they pray too. They can pray for our needs; this kind of prayer for others is called *intercession*. The prayer below asks for healing for our Earth. For what healing would you like to ask the saints to pray?

PRAYER

Blessed are you, Holy Creator,
source of all that is good, beautiful, and whole.
Where wholeness is shattered, goodness damaged or marred,
and beauty bruised or broken, we ask for healing and deep peace.
Be a healing balm for this world:
for all people, creatures, places, events, and for the environment.

We welcome the touch of your healing love and gentle presence.
Inspired by Dorothy Stang, your servant and martyr,
we pray in communion with all the saints in glory,
through Christ our Lord.
Amen.

—Teresita Weind, SNDdeN[18]

ACTIVITY

Test Transpiration

Plants are part of the water cycle through a process called ***transpiration***. Transpiration occurs when water moves out of a plant, mainly through its leaves. There is a lot of transpiration happening in the rainforest.

Materials: Nature Journal, pencil, plastic bag and string or a glass jar or cup.

Instructions: Go outside and find a tree or shrub that is receiving a lot of sunlight. Put your plastic bag around a leafy branch and close the open end of the bag with your string. You can also put a glass jar or cup over grass in a yard or over a potted plant. Check on your covered leaves every half hour. How much water did you collect? Write observations in your Nature Journal. Try covering leaves that aren't in direct sunlight. Which plant transpired the most? Write down your observations.

Make It Rain

In the rainforest it rains more than any other biome! Did you know that you can form rain in a jar?

Materials: empty glass jar, water that has boiled in a pot or teakettle, plate, ice cubes

Instructions: With help from an adult, heat water to boil on your stove. When it is hot enough, pour the water into the jar so it is filled one third of the way. Next, place a plate on top. Wait a few minutes. Now, take ice cubes and place them on top of the plate. Watch as streaks of water run down the jar, making it rain! This is because the moisture in the air from the hot water is cooled and condensed into water droplets. This same thing happens in the atmosphere when it rains. Warm, moist air rises to form clouds. When the colder air in the atmosphere cools the moisture in the clouds, it condenses and falls as rain. Write your observations in your Nature Journal.

Chapter 11

Our Home in the Grasslands

A grassland is an area where the plant life is dominated by grasses. Grasslands may have only a few trees, unlike forests, which may have many trees. Forests are found where there is enough moisture to grow trees. Grasslands are somewhere between a desert and a forest. Deserts are found where there is too little moisture to grow trees. Natural grasslands are maintained by droughts (periods with little rain), fires, seasonal flooding, cutting, or grazing by animals. Without these kinds of disturbance grasslands may change over time into shrublands or forests.

Did you know that grasslands are mentioned in the Bible? They were common in biblical areas, both ***natural*** grasslands and ***cultivated*** grasslands, which were created for farming plants similar to grasses, such as wheat.

NATURE JOURNAL IDEA

Go sit in the grass with your Bible and Nature Journal. Read Mark 6:30–44 and imagine you are there. Write down how you feel. In this passage, Jesus also instructs five thousand listeners to sit in the grass. He uses common things—a few loaves of bread and fish—but multiplies them to feed everyone. He also uses the common items of bread and wine to feed us with himself in the Eucharist. The miracle of the fish and loaves is found in all four books of the Gospel. Do you have an idea why this is so? Write down what you think.

Indigenous peoples of the Great Plains lived in grasslands of North America before they were forced to leave. They are intimately familiar with the grassland ecosystem and the creatures that live there! Many tribes today, such as the Cheyenne River Sioux Tribe, are leaders and models in protecting and restoring prairie grasslands.

Another important crop related to grass and cultivated for food is corn. Corn was first cultivated and farmed by the Indigenous peoples of Mexico thousands of years ago. Corn spread both north and south of Mexico through migration and Indigenous trading networks. Different Indigenous communities grew, and some continue to grow, their own varieties of corn that are important to each culture.

The plains grassland or "prairie grassland" is one of the largest plant communities in North America. Natural grasslands have many different plant species, and therefore, many different animals that depend on them!

Plants of the Grasslands

Big bluestem (*Andropogon gerardii*) Big bluestem is a perennial, warm-season grass native to temperate regions of North America. A ***perennial*** plant is a plant that lives for more than two years, often resprouting from its roots, unlike ***annual*** plants that grow from seeds once a year. Big bluestem is tall and robust, commonly reaching six to eight feet in height. The seed heads have three spikelets that look like a turkey's foot.

Common milkweed (*Asclepias syriaca*) Common milkweed is a flowering plant in the genus *Asclepias*, the milkweeds. Monarch caterpillars feed on milkweed leaves, the only leaves that the monarch caterpillar can eat. Milkweed is

> Sing to the Lord with thanksgiving;
> make melody to our God on the lyre.
> He covers the heavens with clouds,
> prepares rain for the earth,
> makes grass grow on the hills.
> He gives to the animals their food,
> and to the young ravens when they cry.
>
> —Psalm 147:7–9

critical for the survival of monarchs. Without milkweed, monarch butterflies cannot complete their life cycle and their populations decline. Other kinds of milkweed include swamp milkweed (*A. incarnata*) and butterfly weed (*A. tuberosa*). More than 450 species of insects rely on milkweed as a food source. It is so important to plant milkweeds in your garden!

Rattlesnake master (*Eryngium yuccifolium*) The rattlesnake master is a grassland plant of the southeast and midwest United States. It is a member of the carrot family and is planted in many other regions of North America. It has long narrow leaves with spikes and flowers that many people compare to spiky golf balls. Not only is it used by pollinators (bees and butterflies), but Indigenous peoples used its leaves to make shoes. This is one of the oldest examples of shoes made from plants.

Other important grassland plants include coneflowers, asters, and goldenrods. These wildflowers attract many pollinators. In the winter, they provide food and habitat for birds and small animals that feast on the seeds and find shelter in the dried stalks.

Many events in the Bible take place in a garden! Adam and Eve lived in a garden and the tomb where Jesus rose from the dead was in a garden. "Now there was a garden in the place where he was crucified, and in the garden, there was a new tomb in which no one had ever been laid" (John 19:41). Gardens are holy places for life and prayer. If you have a yard, you and your whole family might enjoy creating a garden in it to support plants and animals and provide a special place for prayer.

Blessed Benedict Daswa

The area of South Africa where Benedict lived is savannah, which is like a grassland with some shrubs and trees. Benedict and his wife Eveline had eight children, and Benedict was the principal of the local school and served on the village council. He worked hard to have a fruitful vegetable garden, and he sold its produce, but also gave a lot of vegetables for free to those who needed them. For the children whose families had a tough time paying the tuition for school, he let them pay by working in his garden. Blessed Benedict died as a martyr in 1990.

Animals of the Grasslands

Arthropods

There are many arthropods living in the grasslands of North America. Many pollinators find their homes in grasslands! There are more than four thousand species of native bees in North America. Bees mostly eat and drink pollen and nectar from flowers. They are critically important for pollination. Native bees include mason bees, leaf-cutting bees, and burrowing bees. Native bees are very gentle, but females will sting if you accidentally scare them. Males do not have stingers. It is important to note that most stings are not from native bees, but from honeybees and yellow jackets, which are wasps.

Monarch butterfly (*Danaus plexippus*) The monarch butterfly is a beautiful insect. Its intricate red and black design is very eye-catching! The caterpillar of the monarch butterfly, like many other butterflies and moths, can only eat certain ***host*** plants, in this case, plants in the milkweed family. Host plants are the plants where butterflies and moths lay their eggs. Many other butterflies and moths can be found in grasslands.

Once the caterpillar is large enough, it will become a pupa inside a cocoon before changing into an adult. Some butterflies and moths do not eat anything and will only live for a few weeks, but they might become a tasty snack for a bird!

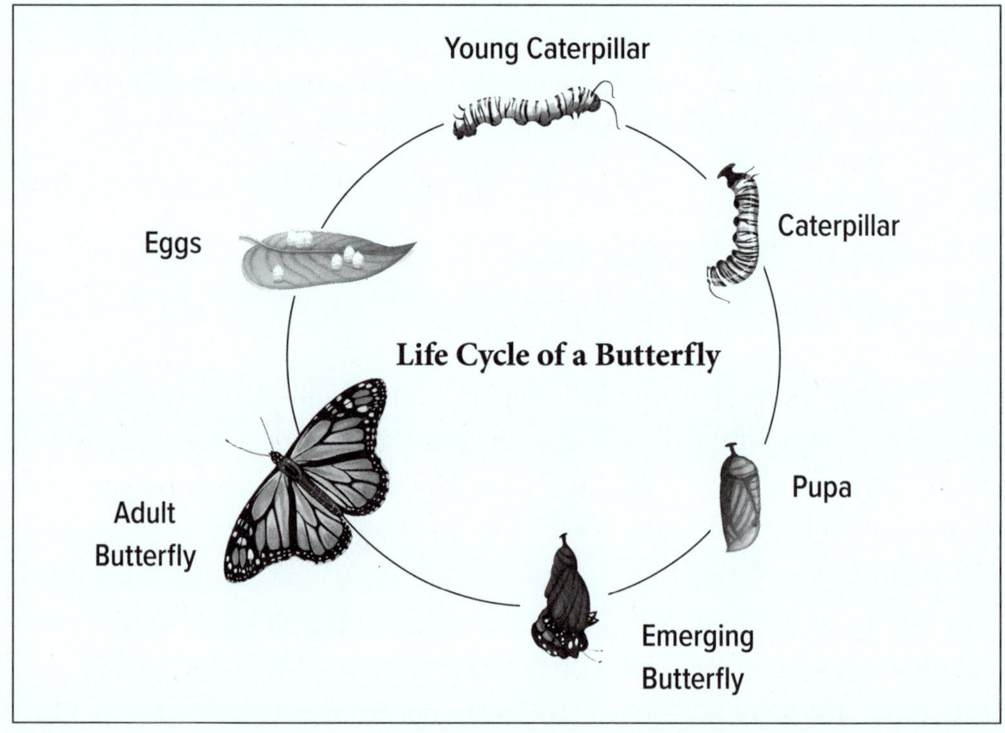

Bumblebees (*Bombus* spp.) Bumblebees are probably the most widely recognized of our native pollen bees. They are also among the hardest working pollinators in the garden. Bumblebees have round bodies covered in soft hair called "pile," making them appear fuzzy. Bumblebees nest underground.

Saint Ambrose of Milan

Bees and beekeepers have a patron saint! Saint Ambrose was a bishop who lived in the fourth century, and he is a Doctor of the Church. His nickname is the "honey-tongued doctor," because his preaching was so good that people loved to listen to him. There is also a legend about Saint Ambrose, that when he was a baby, a swarm of bees landed on his face but did not sting him. Honeybees do swarm (fly in a large group) when they are in search of a new home. If you see a swarm, stay back, and call a local beekeeper from the beekeepers' association.

Birds of the Grasslands

Grasslands are home to a wide variety of birds that require large, open areas of prairie and meadow. Grassland birds may eat insects, seeds, or rodents, all of which are plentiful in a healthy grassland. Grassland birds are adapted to nesting on or close to the ground. They prefer treeless areas because trees provide shelter for predators, such as hawks, skunks, raccoons, foxes, and coyotes.

Eastern and western meadowlarks (*Sturnella magna and S. neglecta*) Meadowlarks sing from fence posts and telephone lines and move through the grasses looking for insects with their long, sharp bills. On the ground, they can be hard to see. But up on perches, they reveal their bright yellow and black chest.

Saint John Chrysostom once said, "The bee is more honored than other animals, not because she labors, but because she labors for others."

Killdeer (*Charadrius vociferus*) The killdeer is a shorebird you can see without going to the beach. You can find them on many kinds of grasslands, including lawns, golf courses, and ball fields. They run across the ground, stopping and then running again, looking for insects. If a predator gets too close to their nest, the killdeer will pretend to have a broken wing to draw the predator away.

American goldfinch (*Spinus tristis*) Male American goldfinches are brilliant yellow and shiny black in the spring. Goldfinches are found throughout much of North America. You can hear their "*po-ta-to-chip*" call when they fly. They are most abundant in areas with thistle and sunflower seeds and near bird feeders.

Other important birds of grasslands include the bobolink, northern bobwhite, horned lark, short-eared owl, red-tailed hawk, and savannah sparrow.

Mammals of the Grasslands

American bison (*Bison bison*) The bison, commonly called buffalo, is the largest land animal in North America. Bison have a hump over their front shoulders and slimmer hindquarters than a buffalo typically found in Africa. Bison have two sharply pointed horns that curve up from the sides of their large heads. Bison graze on grasses, herbs, shrubs, and twigs. Bison have been especially important to Native Americans, who in the past relied on the bison for food and clothing. They used nearly every part of the bison and only hunted what they needed. Now, tribes such as the Assiniboine and the Great Lakota, Dakota, Nakota

Nation are helping to save the bison from extinction by bringing them back to the grasslands. This benefits not only the bison, but also the whole grassland ecosystem.

Coyote (*Canis latrans*) The coyote is a species that belongs to the dog family. Coyotes are smaller than their close relatives, the wolves. They once lived primarily in open prairies and deserts but now also roam North America's forests. Some can be found in and around cities and neighborhoods. Coyotes are omnivores, meaning they will try to eat just about anything.

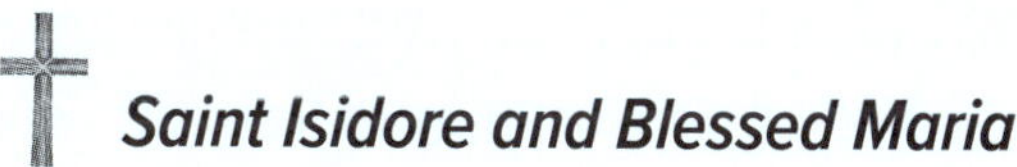

Saint Isidore and Blessed Maria

Farms of corn, wheat, and other grains are a kind of grassland! Saint Isidore the Farmer is the patron saint of farmers and the rural communities that are found far away from cities.

Isidore was born in 1070 to a peasant family near Madrid, Spain. He was a day laborer who worked on the farm of a wealthy landowner. Isidore married Maria Torribia. The couple took a vow to serve God.

Isidore and Maria lived a simple life of charity and faith. They prayed while working and shared what they had with people who were even poorer than themselves. They even shared their meals. Isidore went to Mass early every morning. One day this made him late for work, but when he arrived he saw angels there to help him catch up with his chores.

Isidore and Maria are known for their commitment to family, love for the land, service to the poor, and deep spirituality. They had a great concern for the proper treatment of animals.

NATURE JOURNAL IDEA

Saint Isidore worked hard on a farm every day. Why do you think he chose to go to Mass every morning?

Reptiles and Amphibians of the Grasslands

Garter snake (*Thamnophis* spp.) Garter snakes are small black or brown snakes with yellow stripes on their sides. They are not venomous. Garter snakes are found throughout much of North America. Like all snakes, they are cold-blooded and covered with scales. Snakes cannot see very well and instead rely on their tongues to smell what is around them. As snakes grow, their skin becomes too small and they need to shed it. Garter snakes eat frogs, toads, small rodents, earthworms, spiders, and insects.

American toad (*Bufo americanus*) The common American toad is often seen in or around wetlands during the spring mating season. At other times of the year, it can be found far from water in grasslands, backyards, and gardens. Their colors range from yellow to brown to black, and from solid colors to speckled. Toads eat crickets, earthworms, ants, spiders, slugs, centipedes, moths, and other small ***invertebrates***. (Invertebrates are animals that do not have a backbone, such as arthropods.)

PRAYER

Gardening is a labor of love that lends itself to prayer.

> "Lord, we give you thanks for this great bounty of life entrusted to us. May we be always reminded of your providence, creativity, goodness, and beauty as we tend what you first brought forth. May the complex relationships of people, plants, and animals supported by these gardens spark contemplation of your Holy Trinity, Our Lady's nurturing love, the communion of saints, and the riches of heaven yet to come. Amen."
>
> —Annalise Michaelson[19]

ACTIVITY

Pollinator Poll

The grasslands are important habitats for pollinators. Pollinators not only pollinate plants in the grasslands, but also rely on grasslands for food and shelter so they can be healthy to pollinate plants in other ecosystems.

Materials: Nature journal and pencil; you can also use binoculars and the iNaturalist app.

Instructions: With an adult, go outside to a grassland near you or to a nearby garden. In your Nature Journal record the different kinds of pollinators that you spot. What kinds of plants do you find them on or near? What kind of adaptations do you think they have to help them pollinate? For example, maybe they are furry so that pollen sticks to them. Take pictures of the different pollinators you find in the iNaturalist app. Remember, your observations can help protect these pollinated species of plants and the habitats that rely on them!

ACTIVITY

Find the Grasslands across the World

Materials: Internet access, printer, printer paper, markers.

Instructions: Print out a blackline map of the world. Then use the internet to find out where the grasslands are in South America, Africa, Asia, eastern Europe, and North America. With different colored markers, label these grassland areas on your map. Find out more: How do the grasslands on different continents differ from one another? How are they alike? Are the grasslands in America disappearing? Why?

Chapter 12

Our Home in the Desert

When you think about the Gospel stories of Jesus walking to and from different villages with his disciples, you might imagine him walking along the hot and dry dirt roads of a desert. You might consider the desert to be drab and plain. While it is true that Jesus would have walked through desert areas at times, the landscape would hardly have been plain! If you look closely, a desert is home to some beautiful and unique organisms that are adapted to hot and dry conditions. And the desert is not always hot! Sometimes it can be cold, especially at night. Also, deserts are not always dry. At certain times of the year, they can be wet! During a rainy season, life bursts forth.

Because of its harsh conditions, the desert is mentioned in the Bible as a place of purification. God led the Chosen People through the desert for forty years until they were ready to enter the Promised Land.

The prophet Isaiah foretold the work of John the Baptist, who prepared the people for the coming of Jesus, the Messiah. Isaiah said, "A voice cries out: 'In the wilderness prepare the way of the Lord, make straight in the desert a highway for our God'" (Isaiah 40:3).

Plants that grow only during desert wet seasons are called desert ephemerals. They produce flowers for only a brief period, but these blossoms can be incredibly beautiful, such as the firewheel found in the Sonoran Desert.

Did you know that the Church season of Lent symbolizes the forty days Jesus spent in the desert, fasting and praying, before he began his ministry? During Lent, Catholics make sacrifices and fast like Christ did. We may choose to go without something we enjoy or do something extra during the season to help us grow in holiness as we prepare for Easter.

Another name for the desert in the Bible is the "wilderness." For humans it can be a place of solitude and quiet healing. In such a place, people can learn to let go of distractions and live simply, without luxury, to focus on prayer and their relationship with God.

Also, the desert can be a symbol of hope and persistence. We can look forward with hope to short seasons of relief after periods of suffering. In fact, many biblical passages show that the desert was a place to encounter the living God!

Since the time of Jesus, the desert has been a place of prayer for holy men and women. Many early Christian monks went to the desert of Egypt to live and pray. These men became known as the ***Desert Fathers***.

Saint Anthony of Egypt

Saint Anthony was one of the first Desert Fathers. He lived a very different life from Saint Anthony of Padua, whom you probably know about as the saint who helps you find lost items. This Saint Anthony took to heart the words of Jesus: "go sell your possessions and give the money to the poor . . . then come, follow me." He gave away all his things and went to live by himself in the desert as a hermit, dedicating his time to prayer. We know the story of Saint Anthony because another saint who spent time with him wrote a book about his life.

Either alone as hermits or together as monks, holy people have been seeking out the desert as a place of prayer for hundreds of years. Did you know that even today, there are monks living in the deserts of North America? The Monastery of Christ in the Desert stands today in the wilderness of New Mexico!

North America has four major desert regions. Indigenous peoples, such as the Navajo Nation (the Diné People), the Pascua Yaqui Tribe, and the Mojave Tribe, have lived for thousands of years in North American deserts.

Plants of the Desert

Desert plants are adapted to live in very dry conditions. Plants can store water for long periods of time so that they do not wilt in the heat!

Saguaro cactus (*Carnegiea gigantea*) This cactus is a good example of just how important plants are! The saguaro cactus provides food, shelter, and protection for many desert organisms (see below). When you think of a desert, this cactus is probably what you picture: a giant tree-sized cactus with side-arm structures on each side. This cactus has beautiful blossoms and fruits that are used by other animals. It can live for hundreds of years and store rainwater so it can survive in droughts. Sonoran Desert tribes use saguaro cactus to construct fences, and they harvest the fruit for food, which they eat raw or cook into a sweet syrup.

Desert paintbrush (*Castilleja angustifolia*) This desert wildflower is truly an example of God's masterful handiwork! It is a beautiful plant that thrives in hot and dry

Some species are called ***keystone species***. This means they have so many jobs in an ecosystem that without them, the entire system would collapse. Saguaro cactus is a keystone species.

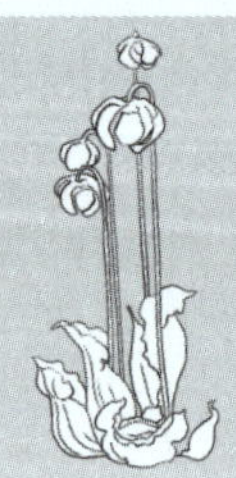

conditions. The paintbrush's flowers are yellow and green, but to attract pollinators like insects and hummingbirds, it has bright red and purple bracts, or casings. Once pollinated, the paintbrush will produce fruits with honeycomb patterned seeds.

✝ *Saint Juan Diego*

Juan Diego lived near what is now Mexico City, Mexico, in the sixteenth century. His name in his native Nahuatl language was Cuauhtlatoatzin, which means "talking eagle." He was given the grace of seeing Mary, the Mother of God. She appeared to him as a young Indigenous woman and asked him to tell the bishop that she wanted a church built there on the hill of Tepeyac. As a sign to the bishop that Juan had really seen her, our Lady told him to pick the flowers at the top of the hill. It was winter, and the desert area was bare and rocky, but Juan found beautiful roses blooming right where Mary said they would be. She arranged them in Juan's cloak, and when he opened his cloak to show the roses to the bishop, an even more amazing sight appeared: an image of Mary miraculously imprinted on the inside of the cloak! Today you can see this very same image of Our Lady of Guadalupe in the shrine in Mexico City.

The Joshua tree (***Yucca brevifolia***) is a plant found in the Mojave Desert. A national park in California was created to protect it and the various species that depend on it—for example, many kinds of birds. Tradition says that the Joshua tree got its name because its branches look like Joshua from the Old Testament lifting his arms in prayer.

Animals of the Desert

The many animals of the deserts of America are tough creatures, able to survive the dry and hot conditions that are found there. Some of these animals can live even with little water and have unique ways of making water last a long time. They may collect morning dew to drink, or have adaptations to their body parts, such as smallness of size; they also use the coolest times of the day to move around.

Arthropods of the Desert

Insects and other desert arthropods have thick exoskeletons to keep the moisture in. They can trap air under their wings to store the moisture that could otherwise be lost in the heat. Many desert insects also come out at night to stay cool.

Desert blonde tarantula (*Aphonopelma chalcodes*) The desert blonde tarantula is found in Arizona and Mexico, in habitats dominated by the saguaro cactus. It has a dark body, with blonde hairs that stand out against it. This spider eats beetles and grasshoppers and other insects that it hunts at night. Watch where you step!

Giant desert hairy scorpion (*Hadrurus arizonensis*) The giant desert hairy scorpion is the largest scorpion in North America, growing up to seven inches long. It is a carnivore that hunts at night. It eats other scorpions, spiders, and snakes. It is dark brown and has yellow claws and legs, a long stinging tail, and many long hairs on its body to detect vibrations, air currents, and chemicals given off by its prey.

NATURE JOURNAL IDEA

Weathering and ***erosion*** are when parts of the Earth's surface, like soil, rocks, and sand, are broken down (weathering) and moved from one place to another (erosion). Water, wind, and even animals can cause weathering and erosion to happen. Although these are natural processes, they happen more often and faster when habitats are harmed. They can occur in any biome, but they occur mostly in the desert because there are few plants. These processes can look like cracked soil, split rocks and sidewalks, or pointed mountaintops. Get outside with your nature journal and draw or record evidence of weathering and erosion near you.

Birds of the Desert

Desert birds make a lot out of a little. During the hottest hours of the day many desert birds hide in the shade and avoid excess flying. Some of these birds can get all the water they need from seeds and other things they eat.

Gila woodpecker (*Melanerpes uropygialis*) Just like the woodpeckers you may see in the forest, the Gila woodpecker nests in holes! These birds create holes in the saguaro cactus, where they lay their eggs. Once they leave the holes, other birds may move in, such as the elf owl. The Gila woodpecker is an omnivore, eating insects, seeds, and even fruits.

Greater roadrunner (*Geococcyx californianus*) "Beep!" One desert bird you may remember from a popular cartoon is the roadrunner. It is true, they are fast! Some are even as fast as an automobile! They eat mostly insects, small reptiles, and rodents but can also eat seeds and fruits. They will even work together in pairs to prey on rattlesnakes. This makes them one of the few predators that rattlesnakes have!

Mammals of the Desert

Desert mammals are very special; they can adapt to the hot weather in many ways. For example, many species of jackrabbit have big, long ears. These ears hold many veins that let their blood cool down as it travels throughout them; this also cools their bodies.

Many mammals will come out only when it is cool—at night, for example. Some desert mammals have less fat than the same species have in the north, and this helps keep them cool.

Mexican long-tongued bat (*Choeronycteris mexicana*) Did you know some bats eat nectar from flowers? These bats are important for the pollination of the saguaro cactus. The cactus blooms for just one night so that these bats can eat the nectar and pollinate the cactus. What a beautiful relationship!

Just as shepherds existed in the time of Jesus, they also exist now in the deserts of North America. In the American southwestern deserts, the Navajo Nation shepherds a rare breed of sheep called the Navajo-Churro sheep. The Navajo have been living in harmony with nature, sustainably grazing their sheep for thousands of years!

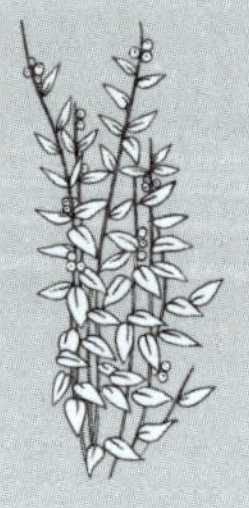

Desert bighorn sheep (*Ovis canadensis*) The desert bighorn sheep gets its name from the males' large horns, which can weigh up to thirty pounds! These sheep are excellent climbers, and this allows them to stay away from predators. The desert bighorn sheep is an herbivore and has a special digestive system that allows it to get extra nutrients out of the plants it eats. This makes it well suited for the desert.

Saint Theonas of Egypt

Saint Theonas was a hermit in Egypt in the fourth century. We know about him because some monks from Jerusalem made a pilgrimage to visit holy monks in Egypt, and one of them wrote an account of the trip.

Theonas stayed in a small hut during the day, keeping silent and praying. People came to ask for his prayers, and he would put his hand out the window to touch them and pray for them. Many people were healed. It is said that at night, when he would leave his hut and go into the desert, wild animals would accompany him. Theonas would draw water from the well for them to drink.

NATURE JOURNAL IDEA

Look around outside to see if there are any places where water has collected, or fill a shallow pan with water. Observe from a distance any birds or other animals who come to drink there. Make note of them in your nature journal.

Reptiles and Amphibians of the Desert

Reptiles do very well in desert conditions, but amphibians have a hard time without water. There are many snakes and lizards in the deserts, but the amphibians are found only in areas close to a stream or other places where there is some moisture. There are plenty of snakes, lizards, toads, and some frogs that live in the desert.

Western diamondback rattlesnake (*Crotalus atrox*) This species of snake is everything you have imagined about a rattlesnake: pointed eyebrows, stern look, and a loud rattler! The western diamondback rattlesnake also has an interesting adaptation: It can use its scales to collect dew from the sand. When it has collected enough, the snake can drink the water, just as it would drink from a pool!

Couch's spadefoot toad (*Scaphiopus couchii*) Couch's spadefoot toad is probably the silliest toad you will ever see. This toad has short legs and a tiny plump body, almost like a cartoon character. These little toads lay eggs in the pools that form after a rain. They also have a "spade" or shovel-like paddle on their hind feet to dig holes in order to hide from predators.

PRAYER

The Desert Fathers are said to have created a very simple prayer that many people use today, known as the Jesus Prayer. It is based on the prayer of the humble tax collector in Luke 18:13. It focuses on using slow, deep breaths to calm your body. With your eyes closed, repeat over and over,

"Lord Jesus Christ, Son of God, have mercy on me, a sinner."

This prayer helps us remember that although we are not perfect, Jesus is always with us, sharing his love and mercy. Like the desert monks, you can feel calm and close to God while praying this way. Although this prayer can be used at any time, you can also use it in the Sacrament of Reconciliation as an ***Act of Contrition***, because it is a prayer to express sorrow for your sins and to ask for forgiveness.

ACTIVITY

Hang with Bats!

Bats are found throughout North America and are important pollinators in both the desert and the tropics. There are many types of bats that live in the desert of the southwestern United States. These bats are adapted to their environment in different ways. Some bats have long tongues for feeding on flowers. Other bats, such as the Mexican free tailed bat, spend summers in large numbers in a cave where they care for their young. Some have large ears like the Townsend's big eared bat.

Most bats also make sounds and then listen to their echoes as they bounce off objects, so they can learn more about their environment. This is called ***echolocation***. These bats have specialized parts of their ears and brains so that they can use these sounds to stay clear of predators and to find food.

Materials: Nature Journal, pencil, blindfold

Instructions: Experiment with echolocation. Ask at least one other scientist to join you to play "Bat and Fly." Choose one person to be the bat. This person will be blindfolded. Everyone else is a fly and can move around. Make sure you are in a space where the blindfolded bat will be safe. All players must walk while playing. The bat will yell "bat" and the flies need to respond "fly." The bat will need to tag each fly.

Take turns being the bat. Record how long it takes each bat to find the flies.

NATURE JOURNAL IDEA

Look up the different species of bats, then write about your favorite. What is its role in the ecosystem?

ACTIVITY

Make Tracks!

Did you know that animal tracks are very visible in the desert? The surface of the desert can be sandy or dusty, and the prints animals make can be very visible. You can even tell the type of animal that was there. Try it at home!

Materials: Nature Journal, pencil, sand (or five cups of flour and one cup of vegetable or baby oil to make sand), baking sheet or large paper plate, small toys or animal figurines that will make good tracks (We like to use lizards!)

Instructions: If you need to make sand, combine five cups of flour with one cup of vegetable or baby oil. Then stir your ingredients until you have a sandy texture. Congratulations, you have sand! Next, spread the sand out on the baking sheet or paper plate. Take the toys and press them into the sand. Can you tell the difference between the animals that you used? What kind of real animal tracks do you think would be the most visible? Perhaps you can find some animal tracks in your yard or a nature area near you. Take a picture of them and, using images you find online, match up the nature tracks with the right kind of animal. If you want to go a step further, use thick cardboard, sponges, or potatoes to make in your sand "footprints" like those you have found outside and/or others you have found online.

Chapter 13

Our Home in the Tundra

A ***tundra*** is a treeless landscape found in cold regions, mostly north of the Arctic Circle and on high mountain tops. Tundra is known for large stretches of bare ground and rock and patchy areas of low vegetation, such as mosses, lichens, herbs, and small shrubs. There are no trees on the tundra because trees cannot handle the harsh conditions and the poor soil.

The tundra is very cold in the winter. The ground is a mix of soil and gravel that is frozen for most of the year. The frozen ground is called ***permafrost.*** During the warm summer, the ground can thaw, giving plants a chance to grow. The growing season is short and stops when the ground freezes again.

Because the cold permafrost will not let roots grow very deep, plants that are shorter and need little or no soil grow the best. The tundra gets only a small amount of rain each year, but plants in the tundra are specially adapted to need only a small amount of water. You can find 1,700 kinds of plants on the tundra, most of which are mosses and lichens.

The tundra is the biome that is the most vulnerable to ***climate change***, caused in part by people. Climate change is the long-term alteration of our temperatures and weather patterns and all the effects of these changes. One impact of warming temperatures in the tundra is the melting of permafrost and ice. This melting disturbs the ecosystem and causes the seas to rise. Climate change comes from having too many ***greenhouse gasses*** in our atmosphere. Greenhouse gasses are gasses like carbon dioxide and methane that trap heat from the sun, making our planet hotter—like a

Indigenous peoples, such as the Inuit, have lived in the tundra for thousands of years. They have close relationships with the animals that live in the tundra and the surrounding ocean, including whales. In the past, whales were hunted for food, and in some communities they are still hunted in a limited way.

greenhouse! Some human activities that create greenhouse gasses are the burning of coal by factories and the use of gasoline in cars. Trees absorb greenhouse gasses and provide us with oxygen. If we cut forests of trees, we have less oxygen and more greenhouse gasses. We can help stop climate change by planting trees and using energy more wisely. In *Laudato Si'*, Pope Francis tells us that people must work together, taking these actions and others. In this way, we can prevent climate change from doing more damage and reverse the damage that has already been done.

Catherine was originally from Russia, but after fleeing from World War I, she ended up in Canada. She formed small communities that still worship God and help the poor today. These communities practice hospitality, welcoming guests to live with them and work together on their farms. Catherine wrote many books and introduced the Russian idea of *poustinia*, which literally means "desert" but refers to a room or small building where one goes to be alone with God in prayer.

Plants of the Tundra

Arctic moss (*Calliergon giganteum*) The frozen soil of the Arctic tundra prevents water from sinking into the ground. During the summer this creates many lakes, streams, bogs, and *fens* (wetlands with high

Did you know that in parts of Alaska there are summer months when it never gets dark? And, in the winter, there are days and days when the sun never rises!

water). Arctic moss is an ***aquatic*** plant that grows in these freshwater lakes and fens. Because Arctic moss can grow under water, it is protected from the wind and the cold, dry air of the frozen tundra.

Reindeer lichen (*Cladonia rangiferina*) Reindeer lichen, also called reindeer moss, is a bushy, branched lichen that covers large areas of the tundra. Reindeer lichen grows in both hot and cold environments. In the tundra this lichen is an important food for caribou (reindeer).

Bearberry (*Arctostaphylos uva-ursi*) Bearberry is a low-growing evergreen shrub. It gets its name because it is a food for bears. Bearberry is adapted to long periods of cold climate, but it also grows in a variety of areas where there is dry, low-nutrient, sandy soil that is exposed to direct sunlight. Bearberry flowers attract bumblebees that pollinate them. Many animals rely on these red berries for food.

Saint Brigid of Kildare

Saint Brigid lived in Ireland in the 400s. As a child, she helped her mother take care of cows on a dairy farm. She was known for giving all she had to the poor, and later she started a monastery. Saint Brigid's feast day is February 1, and in Ireland people celebrate it by making Saint Brigid crosses. They harvest rushes (a wetland plant)

In addition to the arctic fox, other animals that turn white in winter are the snowshoe hare, the peary caribou, and the northern collared lemmings.

and weave them into crosses. Rushes of various kinds are found all over the world, including in the tundra, where they are one of the few species of plants to live!

Animals of the Tundra

Mammals of the Tundra

Caribou (*Rangifer tarandus*) The caribou is a large deer with antlers, also known as reindeer. The dense fur and fat that cover caribou help protect them from the cold. Unlike most mammals, caribou are covered with fur completely. Even their noses are covered! Caribou eat a variety of plants. In the winter, the caribou mostly eat lichens. In the summer, caribou eat lichens, shrubs, mushrooms, and wildflowers, such as lilies, asters, and peas.

Arctic fox (*Vulpes lagopus*) The arctic fox is a small fox with a beautiful white (sometimes blue-gray) coat in the winter. In the summer, the arctic fox has a dark coat. This helps the fox blend in with its surroundings during each season. Arctic foxes eat rodents, birds, and fish. In the winter, when food is hard to find, they follow other animals, like bears, to eat leftover scraps. Foxes will also eat vegetables when these are available.

Saint Albert the Great

Saint Albert the Great lived in the 1200s in Germany and was interested in studying many subjects. Even though he had never visited the tundra, he studied plants and animals where he lived. He understood that animals adapted to their environment, and he once said that if there were bears in the far north, they would be white. In other words, he predicted the existence of polar bears before most people knew they existed!

NATURE JOURNAL IDEA

The writings of Saint Albert the Great contain great wisdom for the People of God. Write about something new you've learned from this field guide. Who would you like to share it with?

Birds of the Tundra

Snowy owl (*Bubo scandiacus*) The snowy owl is a large white owl that spends summers far north of the Arctic Circle hunting lemmings (small rodents), ptarmigan (birds), fish, and other prey. They may eat more than 1,600 lemmings in a single year.

Raven (*Corvus corax*) The raven is a large, all-black bird, related to common crows. Ravens are among the smartest of all birds. They are excellent fliers, even flying upside down! Young ravens play games with sticks, repeatedly dropping them, then diving to catch them in midair.

Most tundra birds are migratory, meaning that they travel to warmer climates in the winter. In the summer many shore birds migrate into the Arctic and depend on the tundra for food.

Insects of the Tundra

Several different types of beetles, weevils, spiders, worms, and other ground-dwelling insects live in the tundra. Many ground insects feed on low vegetation like moss and lichen. The tundra also supports flying insects like mosquitoes, deer flies, blowflies, and even bumblebees.

Arctic wolf spider (*Pardosa glacialis*) The Artic wolf spider is very common in the tundra. Most wolf spiders don't spin webs, but live and feed on the ground. Wolf spiders are predators, and their main source of food are springtails, very small arthropods. These spiders have great eyesight, can camouflage themselves, and are very fast. Like all spiders, they have hairs on their exoskeleton and legs that sense vibrations. All these adaptations make the wolf spider an excellent hunter. Arctic wolf spiders also eat each other!

Arctic mosquito (*Aedes nigripes*) This is the most abundant mosquito in the Arctic tundra. Young mosquitoes grow rapidly in tundra ponds when the snow melts in the early summer. Young mosquitoes eat algae and other tiny organisms in the water. Adult females emerge to drink blood from caribou and other wildlife. Adult males eat nectar from plants. Arctic mosquitoes serve as an important food source for other animals.

NATURE JOURNAL IDEA

Even the most annoying creatures have their place in the ecosystem. Mosquitoes play an important role in the circle of life. Write about some other annoying creatures, living or non-living, and how they do their part for their ecosystem.

Reptiles and Amphibians of the Tundra

Garter snake (*Thamnophis sirtalis*) The tundra is so cold that most reptiles cannot survive there. There is only one kind of snake that can live in the tundra of North America, the garter snake. The garter snake is one of the most common snakes in North America. It is found in the warmer areas of the tundra. The garter snake can withstand low temperatures and can even survive with part of its body frozen!

Wood frog (*Lithobates sylvaticus*) The wood frog is one of only five amphibians that can survive in the cold tundra. The wood frog can sustain life there because it has an antifreeze in its body that prevents it from freezing. In the winter, the wood frog digs into the ground and hibernates (sleeps for the winter).

PRAYER

Cold and chill, bless the Lord;
praise and exalt him above all forever.
Dew and rain, bless the Lord;
praise and exalt him above all forever.
Frost and chill, bless the Lord;
praise and exalt him above all forever.
Hoarfrost and snow, bless the Lord;
praise and exalt him above all forever.
Nights and days, bless the Lord;

praise and exalt him above all forever.
Light and darkness, bless the Lord;
praise and exalt him above all forever.

— Daniel 3:67–72 NABRE

Find Evidence of Life in the Snow

Materials: Nature Journal, pencil, fresh snow

Instructions: When it is snowing, go outside and find impressions in the snow. Do you see footprints? If so, what kind? Do you see other strange shapes or impressions? What makes them? Write or draw your observations in your Nature Journal. Follow the directions on page 132 if you want to make your own tracks in the snow!

Make Fake Snow and Investigate Polar Camouflage

Materials: Nature Journal, pencil, one-pound box of baking soda, one can of shaving cream or a cup of white hair conditioner, large dish or container with a cover, animal figurines of different colors. (If you don't have animal figurines, cut out some pictures of animals from magazines or print them from the internet.)

Instructions: Pour the baking soda into the container. Add some of the shaving cream or hair conditioner and mix it into the baking soda. Keep adding shaving cream or hair conditioner, mixing it in as you go, until the mixture feels like snow. It works well to knead it with your hands. Stop adding shaving cream or hair conditioner when your mixture becomes light and powdery. This can take about ten minutes. When it is fully mixed, it won't leave a sticky mess on your hands. Add some animal figurines to your snow (or lay pictures of different animals on top). Which animals blend best into the snow? Those animals are well camouflaged for polar regions. Enjoy making small snow people or animals with your fake snow. Keep it in a covered container for use at another time. If you want to explore further, follow the directions on page 132 to make your own tracks in your fake snow.

Chapter 14

OUR HOME IN FRESHWATER

The freshwater biome includes small and large bodies of water, such as lakes, rivers, streams, creeks, and wetlands. These bodies of water contain freshwater and are either free of salt or have low salt content. We need this freshwater for drinking, for washing, and for taking care of plants and animals.

People build villages and cities on the banks of rivers to get water for drinking and for watering crops. Water is also useful for traveling by boat.

The writers of the Bible knew how important water is. In the New Testament, water represents new life. We are cleansed of original sin in the sacrament of Baptism. Jesus uses water to remind us to follow him. He describes himself as offering "living water," a way of life that is so fulfilling that no one will be thirsty again (John 4:7–15).

NATURE JOURNAL IDEA

If you can, go to a source of freshwater (such as a brook or spring) with your nature journal and Bible. Read John 7:37–38. How can you help other people who are physically and spiritually thirsty? How can you conserve water?

Only a little of the water on Earth is freshwater. Most of the water is salt water. Much of the freshwater is in the soil or atmosphere or else frozen in ice caps and glaciers. Although only a small amount of freshwater is readily available to us, it is enough water if we use it responsibly and take care of our common home and other people. As the climate changes, water may dry up more often and become harder to find, especially for people who are poor. It is important that we learn to care for water so that people always have enough.

The types of freshwater ecosystems are different from each other depending on the way the water flows. Rivers and streams have ***lotic*** or flowing water that comes together and flows quickly downstream to eventually meet the ocean. Lakes and ponds have ***lentic*** or slow, sometimes standing, and usually deeper water. Wetlands have standing water and are generally very shallow.

Laudato Si' tells us that everything is connected! Freshwater ecosystems are connected within a ***watershed***. A watershed is an area of land where water flows into one common place, such as a river, and then to the ocean. In a watershed, streams flow into rivers and in and out of lakes and ponds, and wetlands border rivers and lakes. In order to keep functioning properly, these ecosystems must be connected.

Plants of Freshwater

Plants growing in or close to the water have special adaptations. They can survive with little air (oxygen) in the soil. Trees, shrubs, and herbs (non-woody plants) that are adapted to freshwater can be found in the water, on the edge of the water, or in the buffer area near the river. Some important herbs of freshwater are cattails, sedges, and swamp mallow. The common reed is an invasive herb that can harm freshwater ecosystems. Cottonwoods, willows, sweetgum, tupelo, and pond pine are trees living in or around freshwater. Many rare, threatened, or endangered plants and animals also live in freshwater ecosystems.

"In considering the fundamental role of water in creation and in human development, I feel the need to give thanks to God for 'Sister Water,' simple and useful for life like nothing else on our planet. Precisely for this reason, care for water sources and water basins is an urgent imperative."

—Pope Francis[40]

Bald cypress (*Taxodium distichum*) The bald cypress is one of many species of trees that live near water. Cypress trees are different from all others in that you can find them living right in the middle of the water in a pond or wetland! They are beautiful, tall trees with wide stumps and thin strips of bark. Bald cypress tress are considered deciduous conifers because they lose their needlelike leaves quickly in the fall, which is why they are called bald. They are native to the southeastern United States, but have been planted in other regions of North America. They can be very old. Some cypress trees are more than one thousand years old! They even have "knees," parts that look like root stubs that stick straight up. Scientists do not know why they have knees.

Mangrove trees (*Rhizophora* spp.) Mangrove trees grow well in and near the water. They have strong roots that cling to the side of the riverbed, allowing them to live as close to the water as possible. Mangroves can grow in freshwater mixed with saltwater, which is called ***brackish*** water. There are many different species of mangroves. Waves splash against the roots of the mangrove tree, making the water calmer while protecting the soil from erosion.

One special type of wetland is called a ***pacosin***. Pacosins are found only on the eastern coast of the United States. They are unique habitats, with unique soil types and pine trees whose cones depend on fire to burst them open and release their seeds! Pacosin is an Indigenous name (in the Algonquin language family) meaning "great marsh."

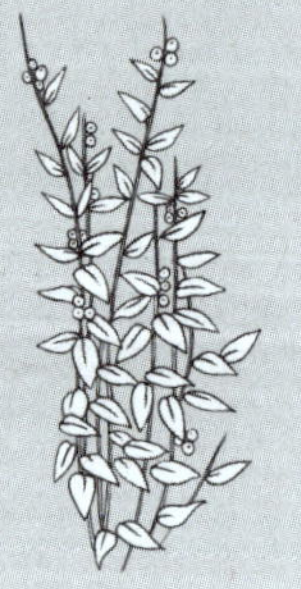

Swamp rose (*Rosa palustris*) Yes, even beautiful roses live in swamps! These roses are pink. They live along riverbanks and even on cypress knees. This rose plant is the host for a kind of moth called a blinded sphinx moth.

American white water lily (*Nymphaea odorata*) You cannot think of freshwater without thinking of the water lily. Flat leaves called lily pads float on the water and serve as resting places for many a frog or dragonfly! The beautiful white flowers open by day and close at night, and the seeds are important food for birds and other animals.

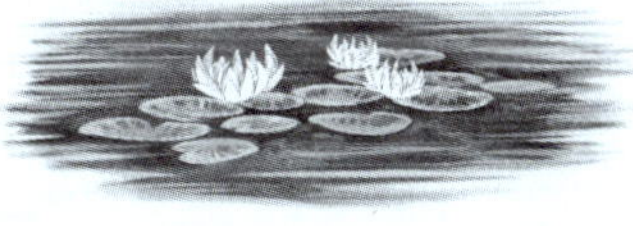

Servant of God Nicholas Black Elk

Nicholas Black Elk was a holy man of the Oglala Lakota people. He was born in 1865 and died in 1950. He became Catholic and a dedicated catechist, a teacher of the Catholic faith. He is called "Servant of God" because the Church has begun the process that will hopefully lead to having him canonized (declared a saint).

Did you know there is a special four-step process to become a canonized saint of the Church? First, the bishop of the place where the person lived begins the process and presents him or her as "Servant of God." Then there is research into that person's past to see if he or she lived a heroically virtuous life. If so, the candidate is given the title "Venerable." For someone to be declared a saint, the Church must prove that two miracles have occurred because of the person's intercession after death. Once one miracle has been investigated and approved, the person is named "Blessed." After a second miracle has been investigated and approved, the person is canonized and declared a saint.

The cottonwood tree has a spiritual significance for many Indigenous peoples. Because the stem of each leaf is flat, the leaves of the cottonwood flutter easily, even when there is little wind. Nicholas Black Elk is said to have pointed to this movement of the cottonwood tree as its "voice" continually praising God.

Animals of Freshwater

Arthropods of Freshwater

Arthropods that depend on freshwater come in all shapes and sizes and have many adaptations. These arthropods include dragonflies, damselflies, and mayflies. There are diving beetles that have special legs shaped like oars to help them swim around! Arthropods may be the most important type of animal in freshwater because they serve as food for many other animals.

Mayfly (*Ephemeroptera* spp.) There are more than six hundred species of mayfly in North America. These insects have thin legs and wings and look like big mosquitoes! But they do not bite. Mayflies, like many other aquatic insects, spend the first part of their lives wingless and under water in streams and ponds. They are an important food source for fish.

Other amazing freshwater creatures include the caddisfly and even the water strider, which is an arthropod but not an insect.

Birds of Freshwater

Birds that live in and around freshwater have different adaptations depending on the type of freshwater ecosystem they live in. There are many freshwater birds to study, such as the belted kingfisher, the pink flamingo, and several types of herons and egrets. Ducks and geese that swim have webbed feet and flat bills for eating aquatic plants and animals. ***Riverine*** birds (which live on or near a river) can swim against the current of the water! There are also many birds that depend on freshwater ecosystems for food but do not do a lot of swimming, such as the red-winged blackbird.

Red-winged blackbird (*Agelaius phoeniceus*) The red-winged blackbird is a marsh bird, meaning that it likes wetlands. These birds build nests in grassy places, such as in the midst of cattails or in weedy fields. They have a unique call (*GUR-ga-lee!*) and the males are entirely black except for their beautiful red and orange shoulder stripes. The females look very different—they are mostly brown, with lighter brown streaks.

American dipper (*Cinclus mexicanus*) This little bird lives in the mountains throughout the western portion of North America, from Central America to the Rocky Mountains, up through Alaska. It looks like a normal songbird but can dive and swim in fast-flowing rivers. It can close its nostrils and has an extra eyelid to see underwater. It eats insects, such as the ***larvae*** (immature forms) of dragonflies. It also eats tadpoles.

Common loon (*Gavia immer*) Loons are beautiful birds that live near the lakes of North America. They are diving birds that search for fish to eat, such as the sunfish. Loons have the same shape as ducks, but their necks are longer. Their feet are webbed, as ducks' feet are. Their call is an eerie, yet beautiful, song that rings out over the lake in the evenings. The loon is a star in many Native American writings and stories.

Father Gerard Manley Hopkins

Gerard was born in England in the nineteenth century. He became Catholic, and then he became a Jesuit priest. All his life he wrote poetry. He used lovely images from nature to write about God. Only after his death did he become famous for his poems. He wrote a beautiful one, called "As Kingfishers Catch Fire," in which he connected the beauty of this freshwater bird with the presence of Christ.

NATURE JOURNAL IDEA

Describe the freshwater biome or another favorite biome in a poem. Use details to explain what makes this biome beautiful and unique.

Or: Pick a beautiful freshwater creature. Describe it in writing—either from your personal experience or from research in the library or online.

Mammals of Freshwater

Mammals living in or near freshwater have adaptations to keep them warm, such as thick fur. The river otter and moose are important freshwater mammals. Other adaptations of freshwater mammals include webbed feet and strong tails to help in swimming.

Springs, where water flows from the ground, are important in the history of our Catholic faith. People have been baptized at springs with spring water—as Saint Kateri was! In the apparition of Mary in Lourdes, France, a spring bubbled from the Earth. Many people have been healed of their sicknesses by the water from this spring, which is still flowing.

American beaver (*Castor canadensis*) Did you know that beavers are very important for the overall health of freshwater habitats? Beavers are rodents, like mice and rabbits. They use their teeth to chop down small trees. Then with the loose branches they build dams on rivers or streams. These dams create pools where beavers can make their homes in lodges or dens. The entrances are under water, making these beaver homes safe places to have and care for their babies. Other freshwater animals can live in the same pools. By damming rivers and streams, beavers also create wetlands.

Moose (*Alces alces*) Moose are also important for freshwater habitats and the land that surrounds them. Moose are herbivores and help keep a healthy balance of plants in freshwater ecosystems. Moose poop and pee also help some land ecosystems! When moose eat aquatic plants they take in their nutrients, such as nitrogen, and leave nitrogen and other nutrients on the soil when they pee and poop. This helps land plants grow.

NATURE JOURNAL IDEA

Human beings are "wired" to live in community with others. However, some people are called by God to live as hermits and dedicate their lives to prayer and penance. Today, modern-day hermits usually live alone, but

Did you know that a rodent's teeth never stop growing? It's true! Rodents like beavers keep their teeth from getting too long by chewing on trees and other wood.

they are obedient to their local bishops and they pray for the needs of other people and the whole world. These hermits have the opportunity to immerse themselves in nature. What do you think it would be like to live as a hermit? What would make this life easier? What would make it harder?

Reptiles and Amphibians of Freshwater

There are many species of turtles and snakes that live in and around freshwater. You have probably walked by them without noticing because of their camouflage! These reptiles love to sit on rocks in ponds or rivers with the warm sun on their backs. They eat small fish.

Amphibians are small ***vertebrates*** (animals with backbones) that need water or at least a moist environment to survive. They include frogs, toads, salamanders, and newts. One unique freshwater amphibian is the hellbender, a rare large-stream salamander. Tree frogs, amphibians that live on land as adults, have suction cup feet for climbing trees. Other amphibians that live in water have webbed feet for swimming and an extra eyelid to help with seeing underwater.

Alligator snapping turtle (*Macrochelys temminckii*) Snapping turtles can be scary, with their big jaws and eyes. Do not worry, they are more afraid of you than you are of them! They can bite, so it is best not to try to touch them. These amazing turtles look the same now as they did millions of years ago. They have a long tail and a pointed nose that they use to stick out of the water in order to breathe. They lay eggs shaped like ping pong balls in the ground near rivers and streams. Alligator snapping turtles are the largest freshwater turtles in the world!

American bullfrog (*Lithobates catesbeianus*) There are many species of frogs that live in fresh water. You may know the most common, bullfrogs. These are large frogs that make low croaking sounds. You can find them sitting on lily pads or on the edges of a pond in the summer.

Fish of Freshwater

Freshwater fish are amazing animals that are important for humans. People catch fish to eat or to catch and release them for fun. Some types of freshwater fish include trout, sunfish, darters, and bass.

Saint Peter the Apostle

During the time of Jesus, several of his disciples made their living by catching and selling freshwater fish. The first two fishermen Jesus called were Simon and his brother Andrew. Jesus gave Simon a new name, Peter. Peter means "Rock," because Simon Peter would become the leader of the Church—the rock on which Jesus built his Church.

Jesus used fish as a symbol for his ministry, saying "Follow me, and I will make you fish for people" (Matthew 4:19). The Sea of Galilee is the freshwater lake where Jesus walked on water and where his disciples fished. This lake in Israel is also called the Sea of Tiberius or Lake Gennesaret.

Brook trout (*Salvelinus fontinalis*) Trout are some of the most beautiful fish. Different species of trout live in streams throughout North America. One of the most famous species is the brook trout. People love to catch them to see their beauty up close. Often they release them to catch another day. For these trout to survive, they need clean water, plenty of insects to eat, and shade to keep the water cool. This is one of the reasons it is important to have healthy forests along streams.

Bluegill sunfish (*Lepomis macrochirus*) Bluegill sunfish are found throughout North America. They can be a variety of colors, but all have one black spot on their upper fins. They are also distinguished from other sunfish because of their small mouth and black earflap. They are carnivores with a diverse diet; they eat insects, worms, fish eggs, shrimp, crayfish, and more.

PRAYER

All-powerful God, you are present in the whole universe
and in the smallest of your creatures.
You embrace with your tenderness all that exists.
Pour out upon us the power of your love,
that we may protect life and beauty.
Fill us with peace that we may live
as brothers and sisters, harming no one.

—Pope Francis, *Laudato Si'*[21]

ACTIVITY

Compare a Clear and a Muddy River

Materials: Nature Journal, pencil, two jars, small shovel, a creek or river

Instructions: First, use the shovel to scoop the top layer of sediment from the river or creek bed and place it in one of the jars. Add river water and seal the jar tightly. Fill the second jar with water, scoop a deeper layer of sediment, and place it in this second jar. Seal it tightly. In your Nature Journal, note which jar has larger versus smaller particles of sediment.

Next, flip your jars over. In which jar does it take longer for the pieces of sediment to reach the bottom? What is the dominant type of sediment in each jar? Record your observations in your Nature Journal.

Note that the smaller the pieces of sediment, the longer they take to reach the bottom. This is what makes some rivers clear, and others muddy! Muddy rivers have riverbeds with silt and clay, very small particles. They tend to stay in the water and don't always reach the bottom! Clear rivers have more gravel and cobble. These streams support trout and other fish that like to nest among the stones.

ACTIVITY

Compare Freshwater and Saltwater Organisms

Materials: Nature Journal, pencil, internet source on computer or phone.

Instructions: Choose a freshwater organism, perhaps one listed in this book. Look it up on the internet. Draw a picture of it in your Nature Journal. If you can, safely observe it live, in nature. Write a list of its unique features. Now choose a saltwater organism. Look it up and draw a picture of it. If you can, safely observe it live, in nature. Write a list of its unique features. How are the organisms the same? How are they different? What features do they have that make them well adapted for the environment they live in? If you want to go one step further, research one organism that thrives in muddy environments and compare and contrast it with your other findings!

Chapter 15

OUR HOME IN SALTWATER

The aquatic, or water, biomes are the largest of all the biomes on Earth. Water biomes can be either freshwater or saltwater (marine). Freshwater, as in lakes and rivers, has a low salt concentration. Salt is a mineral found in rocks; it dissolves in water. Saltwater, as in oceans and estuaries, has a higher concentration of salt. Estuaries are the mouths of rivers that empty out into the sea. In estuaries freshwater and saltwater mix.

A wide variety of plants and animals live in and around saltwater.

The ocean (usually called the "sea") is mentioned in many parts of the Bible. It is often described as something dangerous and intimidating. But the greatness of the sea gives glory to God, who made it.

The book of Exodus describes how God led the Chosen People through the sea in order to escape from slavery in Egypt. This event is central to the story of God's dealings with his people. It is mentioned many times throughout the Bible.

The book of Jonah tells the story of a prophet who didn't want to go where God sent him. Jonah tried to run away from God by getting on a boat heading in the opposite direction. In the story, God causes a great storm on the sea. In order to save the other sailors, Jonah lets them throw him into the sea, knowing that he is the cause of the storm. God then sends a "large fish" (Jonah 1:17) to swallow Jonah and spit him up on the shore. Having learned his lesson, Jonah is now ready to go preach where God tells him to!

Our Lady Star of the Sea

In the Catholic tradition, many people have devotion to Our Lady Star of the Sea. People who sail and work on the sea ask Mary to pray for them, protect them, and make sure they get home safely. Many churches in North America, particularly near the coast, are named after Our Lady Star of the Sea, in Latin, *Stella Maris*. Pictures of

Mary, Star of the Sea show her with boats and lighthouses, because Mary is said to guide people home.

Blessed Niels Stensen

Niels was a scientist in seventeenth-century Denmark. He was interested in anatomy, which examines the bodies of humans and other animals. One day he examined the head of a dead shark and noticed that the teeth were like the stony objects found in certain rocks. He realized that those objects had not grown in the rocks or dropped from the sky, as some people said, but that they were fossils of teeth from sharks that lived long ago. This meant that those rocks had once been under the ocean. Niels is the scientist who came up with the principle that layers in rocks represent periods of time, with the lower layers being older than the upper layers. This is why he is called the "father of modern geology." Niels became Catholic as a young man, and later was ordained a priest and then a bishop.

Plants and Algae of Saltwater

Common eelgrass (*Zostera marina*) Common eelgrass is a marine flowering plant that grows in cooler waters near the shore. This type of seagrass provides food and habitat for many kinds of fish and other marine organisms.

Kelp (*Laminaria* spp.) Kelp is a large brown alga that is a kind of seaweed. Kelp forests provide an important habitat for a variety of fish and other marine organisms. There are about thirty species of kelp.

Green algae (*there are too many kinds of species in this group of organisms to list one generic name*) Green algae contain chlorophyll, which gives them a bright green color. Chlorophyll absorbs light, which helps to make food for algae and other plants. There are about six thousand species of green algae.

Animals of Saltwater

Arthropods of Saltwater

Lobsters (*Homarus* spp.) Lobsters are marine arthropods that live on the bottom of the ocean and on the coastline. They live in burrows, seagrasses, and the holes between rocks. They have five pairs of legs. Some lobsters have claws or pinchers on their legs. They can be many different colors, but their blood is clear. They are omnivores, eating algae, plants, shrimp, fish, worms, and other arthropods. They use hairs on their legs to "smell" food.

Barnacles (*Cirripedia*) Barnacles are small marine arthropods that can attach themselves to almost anything—even other barnacles. They like to attach themselves to something that is active, like underwater volcanoes, whales, and boats. Barnacles have a soft body, but they create a hard casing around themselves that they can open or close depending on threats and changing water levels. When their casing is open, they use their small legs for eating.

Birds of Saltwater

Double-crested cormorant (*Nannopterum auritum*) Sea birds are adapted to life within the marine environment. Double-crested cormorants are large, dark waterbirds with small heads on long, kinked necks. Cormorants are experts at diving underwater to catch small fish. They can be found standing on docks and rocks holding their wings out to dry.

American avocet (*Recurvirostra americana*) American avocets can be found on both the Atlantic and Pacific coasts and other habitats with shallow water. They are large shorebirds with long legs and a long bill. They use their bill to scan the water and locate food through touch. Their bodies are white and their wings are black with a white stripe. Their heads and necks change color; in the winter they are red and in the summer they are white or light gray.

NATURE JOURNAL IDEA

The shape and size of bird beaks are adapted to the kind of food each species eats. On the coast, many birds have beaks that are shaped like tweezers so they can pick out animals that are burrowing in the sand. Some tweezer beaks are longer than others and can go deeper into sand. Other birds have beaks shaped like a big spoon or ladle so they can scoop food out of the water. You can find many species of birds eating at the shore at the same time because they eat different things. Go outside with your nature journal and draw or record the types of beaks you see and what each beak is being used to eat.

Mammals of Saltwater

Toothed whales (*Odontoceti* spp.) Toothed whales are marine mammals with teeth. This category includes several species of whales, dolphins, and porpoises. The sperm whale (*Physeter macrocephalus*) is the largest of the toothed whales. They can grow to about sixty feet long and weigh as much as 130,000 pounds. The orca (*Orcinus orca*) is easily recognized by its striking black and white markings. Orcas can grow to about twenty-six feet long and weigh as much as 22,000 pounds. Orcas can live up to sixty years.

Corals are animals! They are tiny invertebrates that live together in a colony, usually in tropical waters, although deep-water corals exist in colder water. They are a keystone species that is greatly affected by climate change and habitat destruction. There is a coral reef off the coast of Florida named after a saint, the St. Lucie coral!

If you want to fish in freshwater or saltwater you need a fishing license. You can buy a fishing license at a sporting goods store or online. It allows you to fish and helps scientists keep track of how many people are fishing. That way, we can make sure that enough fish live, and we all can continue to fish for years to come! Fishing so that there are enough fish for the future is called ***sustainable*** fishing.

Baleen whales (*Mysticeti* spp.) Baleen whales do not have teeth. They use baleen, which is made of keratin, the same material that is in our fingernails, to filter water as it enters their mouth. There are fourteen species of baleen whales, including the humpback, gray, blue, and fin whales. Most baleen whales are larger than toothed whales. The largest baleen whale is the blue whale. It can reach ninety-eight feet in length and weigh over 400,000 pounds.

Fishes and Mollusks of Saltwater

Striped bass (*Morone saxatilis*) Striped bass is a fish found along the Atlantic coast of North America. They have silvery bodies with long black stripes. The largest striped bass weighed 124

In early Christianity, Christ was symbolized by a fish. The Greek word for "fish," ἸΧΘΥΣ (ichthus), is spelled using the first letters of the phrase "Jesus Christ, God's Son, Savior."

One of the most beautiful things about the shore of the ocean is the many types of seashells. Seashells are the leftover exoskeletons of invertebrates like clams and snails. These shells are mostly made of calcium carbonite and can be many different colors and shapes, even perfect spirals. When they wash up on the shore, they are like tiny treasures from God. When we look at them, we are reminded of the beauty of God's creation. Even the broken shells can be beautiful.

pounds. Don't be fooled, striped bass can live in freshwater too! They swim up into freshwater rivers to spawn.

King or chinook salmon (*Oncorhynchus tshawytscha*) King salmon is the largest salmon on the Pacific coast of North America. These salmon are blue-green on top with silvery sides and white bellies. They hatch in rivers, swim out to the saltwater ocean to live and grow, and return to the same freshwater rivers to lay their eggs or "spawn." King salmon can weigh more than one hundred pounds.

Scallops (*Pectinidae* spp.) Scallops are a clam-like animal. There are many species of scallops, all of which are only found in salt water, not in fresh water. Scallops can swim! They use jet propulsion by quickly opening their valves to draw water in and then pushing the water out. This helps them to move forward. They swim when they sense danger, such as sea stars, which like to eat scallops.

Saint James the Greater and the Scallop Shell

Scallop shells are used as a symbol of the sacrament of Baptism, and a symbol of ***pilgrimage***, which is a journey to a holy place. It is interesting to see how these two things are connected.

Saint James the Greater was one of the twelve apostles, the brother of Saint John. (There was also another apostle named James; he is called Saint James the Lesser.) In Spain there is a large church dedicated to Saint James the Greater. It is believed that he was buried there, and for hundreds of years many people have been traveling there on pilgrimage. The name of this pilgrimage is el Camino de Santiago (the Way of Saint James). Since scallops are abundant along the coast of this part of Spain, pilgrims would bring back a scallop shell as a sign that they had completed their pilgrimage. Eventually, the scallop symbol became associated with people going on any kind of pilgrimage.

Since Baptism is the beginning of our life-long pilgrimage to heaven, the scallop shell also symbolizes Baptism, and you can sometimes see the priest or deacon using a scallop shell to pour water on the person being baptized.

NATURE JOURNAL IDEA

Some of the most popular sites of Catholic pilgrimages include Vatican City in Rome, the Holy Land in Israel, and the places where Mary has appeared, such as Lourdes in France, Fatima in Portugal, and the Basilica of Our Lady of Guadalupe in Mexico. Saint Kateri has two national shrines in North America: one in the United States and one in Canada. Where would you like to go on a pilgrimage? Why? Write about it.

Reptiles of Saltwater

Sea turtles (*Dermochelyidae and Cheloniidae* spp.)

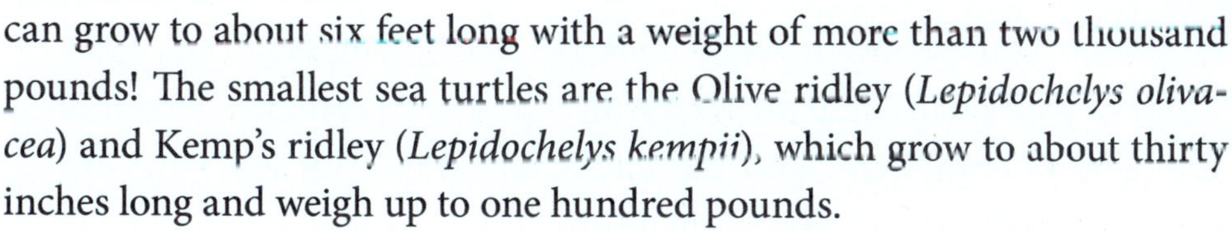

Sea turtles are marine reptiles. Although they live in the sea, they need air to breathe, as all reptiles do. There are seven species of sea turtle. The leatherback (*Dermochelys coriacea*) is the largest. Leatherbacks can grow to about six feet long with a weight of more than two thousand pounds! The smallest sea turtles are the Olive ridley (*Lepidochelys olivacea*) and Kemp's ridley (*Lepidochelys kempii*), which grow to about thirty inches long and weigh up to one hundred pounds.

American crocodile (*Crocodylus acutus*) The American crocodile is a long, lizard-like reptile. It has a long tail and short legs. Males can reach twenty feet in length and weigh up to 840 pounds. While its front feet have five toes, its back feet only have four toes. The American crocodile has a triangular snout. Its nostrils, eyes, and ears are positioned at the top of its head, so that the crocodile can stay beneath the surface of the water and still smell, see, and hear.

PRAYER

Dear Mary, Star of the Sea,
With your light of love and holy care
guide us on the sea of life.
Hold us steady in times of storm,
and comfort us when we feel alone.
Help us to follow Jesus as you did,
with pure and faithful hearts,
trusting always in the goodness of God. Amen.

—Patricia Szczebak

ACTIVITY

Create Your Own Tidepool

Materials: Nature Journal, pencil, recycled tray or pan, sand (you can make your own, using the recipe on page 132), pebbles, a container to put water in, water, and any "beach and sea organisms" (toys or representations you have on hand).

Instructions: Create a beach inside of your tray using the pebbles and sand. Add your "organisms." If possible, go outside with your "beach" and a full container of water. Make high and low tide by varying water levels inside the tray. First add just a small amount of water to create a low tide. Then add more water to create a high tide. Record which of your "species" are exposed during low tide and which ones are exposed during high tide. Also record how high tide affects the whole area. If you have sand in your tray, you may also witness some erosion!

ACTIVITY

Observe the Tides

Materials: Nature Journal, pencil, area tide chart found in the newspaper or on the internet.

Instructions: Choose an area of the shore and observe it at different tidal times. Draw or photograph what you see. Add your pictures to your Nature Journal. Record any other observations you have of tidal changes in that area. If you can, compare your observations to the information found in the tide chart for that same area.

Chapter 16

WHAT YOU CAN DO

In this book you have explored how our Catholic faith teaches us to care for our common home, the Earth, and all the creatures in it.

You learned that people are a special part of nature, not separate from it. God has made us responsible for taking care of creation.

You have heard from saints, popes, priests, sisters, nuns, brothers, Catholic scientists, and monks. You learned about some of the beautiful species that inhabit our planet and the special homes they live in—biomes, ecosystems, and habitats. You learned about what the Bible tells us about nature, and how the great prophets and Jesus, God the Son, used the natural world to tell stories and teach lessons. You even learned that the Eucharist, which has truly become Jesus during the Mass, is first made from products of the Earth—wheat and grapes.

Now that you know and understand all these things, it is time to learn what you can do! That is right, you can make a difference!

Our home on Earth is threatened. Many times, people do not use the Earth's resources responsibly. Sometimes we cut down too many trees without replacing them, or pave too many roads that change and destroy habitats, and we forget to think about how our actions impact the environment we need to survive.

Thankfully, there are many things you can do to help. Here are a few to get you thinking—and taking action:

Go to Mass regularly. Mass is the highest form of prayer. Communion with Jesus and the people of God gives us strength and peace. Offer your prayers at Mass for the protection of our Earth and all the people that depend on it!

Pray every day. Ask God to help people to make the right choices to protect our Earth. Pray for the poor, who depend on the Earth's resources to survive. Learn to pray the Rosary or other traditional Catholic prayers. Pray in your own words or pray just by being quiet, aware of the presence of God. There are many, many ways to pray.

Ask Mary, Saint Francis, Saint Kateri, or another saint to pray for you. There is a patron saint for every activity and for every interest. Your patron saint can be the saint of your birthday or Baptism day, or a saint that has the same name as you. The saints in heaven who are enjoying the sight of God will pray for us if we ask them. Their prayers are meaningful because they are close to God. You are part of the communion of saints, and their intercession is a special gift.

Go outside. Learn what species are in your yard and at your school, park, and parish. Studies have shown us that spending time outside is good for human beings in many ways. Get out there and be a part of nature, God's wonderful creation!

Welcome the native insects that come into your yard and garden. Animals and bugs are good! They live in certain areas because they have a role to play in the ecosystem. We need them for our natural world to be healthy! Did you know that an oak tree is the best tree to plant because thousands of species of insects depend on oaks?

Learn. Read the Bible. Read books. Read the "book of nature" outside. Work hard in school. The more you learn about nature, the more you will enjoy it, understand it, and know how to conserve it. The more you learn about and grow in faith, the closer you will be to God, the Creator of all! You can find more books about the saints and Catholicism at the Pauline Books and Media website (which can be found on the Resources page, 177).

Play and have fun too! The outdoor world is like a playground, made for us to enjoy and care for. (But be sure to follow the safety guidelines on page 3.)

Plant something! Plant native plants—a tree, flowers, or a whole garden. In this field guide you learned about native plants—plants that evolved in each of the biomes on Earth. You can plant native plants in your yard, school, park, or parish. Maybe your parents or guardians can buy native plants at a special nursery or online. Many famous saints tended gardens and plants where they lived.

Plant a Mary Garden. At the Saint Kateri Conservation Center website, you can learn what to plant in a ***Mary Garden***, a garden that symbolizes our Lady. For example, blue flowers represent our Lady's clothes. There are many native blue plants with blue blossoms. (This website can be found on the Resources page, 177.)

Plant a vegetable garden. Growing a vegetable garden is a fun and healthy way to learn to love the land! Many churches plant vegetable gardens and donate the food to people who are poor. Ask your pastor if your church has a vegetable garden.

Download the iNaturalist app on a smartphone and take pictures to learn and record what you see. The more you learn, the more you can understand how to help each creature! You can find information about the iNaturalist app on the Resources page 177.

Learn about Indigenous peoples. Many of these peoples were forced to leave their original homes and now live somewhere else in their country. You can learn which tribes live where you live and explore their histories and ancestral lands.

Register your backyard garden habitat (or parish, school, or community garden) as a Saint Kateri Habitat! At the Saint Kateri Conservation

Center, we have a special program to teach people how to care for creation in their yard, so others will learn to care for creation too! Learn more and register your habitat at the website (Resources page, 177).

Reduce, re-use, recycle! You can help the world by reducing the amount of trash you create. Reuse items as much as you can. Choose reusable items like water bottles and containers for your lunches at school. If you have to use plastic items or other disposable items, make sure to recycle them!

Save energy. When you are not in a room, turn off the lights. Unplug appliances and devices when they are not in use. Use heat and air conditioning wisely. This helps to reduce climate change.

Save water. You can help to save water by using only what you need. Turn the water on and off when you are brushing your teeth. You can build a rain garden that helps to clean the water that comes from the roof of your home! Learn more about how to conserve water by researching on the internet with your parent or guardian.

Be thankful for all the good things you have and all the wonderful creatures in the world! Say a prayer of gratitude every day, thanking God for all his good gifts in the natural world and in your life.

PRAYER

Dear God,

Thank you for the beautiful world that you created. Thank you for the air and water, trees and bugs, birds and elephants, vegetables and flowers, pets and polar bears. Thank you for all the living creatures, each here on Earth for a reason.

Thank you for my life. I know that every breath I take is a gift from you. I am unique. There has never been another person just like me, and there will never be another person just like me. Guide me as I learn the purpose you have for my life and help me to live according to your will.

Thank you for all human life. Thank you especially for the people who help me and love me. Thank you for the lives of my family and friends.

I am sorry for the times that I have not appreciated all the gifts that you have given me, for the times I have not loved the people in my life as I should, and for the times I misused or wasted the gifts of the Earth. I am sorry for the times I have not given you the worship and praise you deserve. I ask for your forgiveness.

I pray for the people that I know need help, and I pray for my own needs. (Say what you would like to pray for here.)

I love you, Lord, today and always.

I offer this prayer in the name of the Father, Son, and Holy Spirit.

Amen.

RESOURCES

We've done our best to find trustworthy sources of information to aid your exploration, but websites can change. It's always a good idea to talk about any questions you might have after researching and learning new things. Some websites are for kids, but others were created for grownups, so we recommend that kids and grownups explore these resources together. Be media smart, and enjoy learning more about how scientific study and faith in God can both help us to grow in true wisdom and appreciation for the natural world.

Catechism of the Catholic Church

You can read this online through the U.S. Catholic bishops: https://www.usccb.org/sites/default/files/flipbooks/catechism/, or through the Vatican: https://www.vatican.va/archive/ENG0015/_INDEX.HTM

iNaturalist app

A cell phone application with which you can record observations of plants and animals and share them with others. For more information, see https://www.inaturalist.org/, and download the free smart phone app from your usual app store. (For a minor to create an account, an adult needs to give consent and verify their identity by using their credit card to donate at least $1.)

Laudato Si'

You can read this online through the Vatican: vatican.va (at the top righthand corner, choose "English" for the language and search by title for this encyclical of Pope Francis)

Also available as a print copy from Pauline Books and Media.

Mary Garden

For ideas on planting a Mary Garden: www.kateri.org/mary-gardens-for-a-spiritual-experience/

Pauline Books and Media

The publishing house of the Daughters of St. Paul, the publishers of this book. Find more books for kids on faith, saints, science, and prayer. paulinestore.com

Saint Kateri Conservation Center

A national Catholic conservation group that promotes faith, integral ecology, and the diversity of life. www.kateri.org

HOW TO PRAY THE ROSARY

The Rosary is a Catholic prayer that is prayed using rosary beads. When we pray the Rosary, we say prayers as we follow the beads, such as the Lord's Prayer (Our Father) and the Hail Mary. A person who prays the Rosary thinks about certain events from the Bible while praying. These events are called the ***Mysteries of the Rosary.***

1. Make the Sign of the Cross; then pray the Apostles' Creed while holding the crucifix.
2. Pray the Our Father while holding the large bead next to the crucifix.
3. Pray three Hail Marys while touching the three small beads that follow. Pray the Glory.
4. Name the mystery; then pray the Our Father on the large bead.
5. Pray ten Hail Marys, using the small beads to keep count. Pray the Glory.

Repeat steps four and five for each mystery.

6. When you reach the end, pray the Hail, Holy Queen.
7. Make the Sign of the Cross and kiss the crucifix.

1. Make the Sign of the Cross and pray the Apostles' Creed.
2. Pray the Our Father.
3. Pray 3 Hail Marys.
4. Pray the Glory Be, name the first Mystery, and pray the Our Father.
5. Pray 10 Hail Marys.
6. Pray the Glory Be, name the second Mystery, and pray the Our Father.
7. Repeat steps 5 and 6 with each Mystery until you reach the end.
8. Pray the Glory Be and the Hail, Holy Queen.
8.
4.
5.
3.
2.
1.
6.
7.

ROSARY PRAYERS

(When the Rosary is prayed in a group, the leader prays the words in italics.)

Sign of the Cross

In the name of the Father, and of the Son, and of the Holy Spirit. Amen.

Our Father

Our Father, who art in heaven, hallowed be thy name. Thy kingdom come, thy will be done on earth as it is in heaven. Give us this day our daily bread, and forgive us our trespasses, as we forgive those who trespass against us. And lead us not into temptation, but deliver us from evil. Amen.

Hail Mary

Hail Mary, full of grace, the Lord is with thee. Blessed art thou amongst women, and blessed is the fruit of thy womb, Jesus. Holy Mary, Mother of God, pray for us sinners now and at the hour of our death. Amen.

Glory Be

Glory to the Father, and to the Son, and to the Holy Spirit; as it was in the beginning, is now, and will be for ever. Amen.

The Apostles' Creed

I believe in God, the Father almighty, Creator of heaven and earth,
and in Jesus Christ, his only Son, our Lord,
who was conceived by the Holy Spirit, born of the Virgin Mary,
suffered under Pontius Pilate, was crucified, died, and was buried;
he descended into hell;
on the third day he rose again from the dead,

he ascended into heaven,
and is seated at the right hand of God the Father almighty;
from there he will come to judge the living and the dead.
I believe in the Holy Spirit,
the holy catholic Church,
the communion of saints,
the forgiveness of sins,
the resurrection of the body,
and life everlasting. Amen.

Hail, Holy Queen

Hail, holy Queen, Mother of mercy, our life, our sweetness, and our hope. To you do we cry, poor banished children of Eve; to you do we send up our sighs, mourning and weeping in this valley of tears. Turn then, most gracious advocate, your eyes of mercy toward us; and after this our exile, show unto us the blessed fruit of your womb, Jesus. O clement, O loving, O sweet Virgin Mary.

THE MYSTERIES OF THE ROSARY

The Joyful Mysteries

Usually prayed on Mondays and Saturdays.

1. The Annunciation of the Archangel to Mary
2. The Visitation
3. The Nativity
4. The Presentation in the Temple
5. The Finding of Jesus in the Temple

The Luminous Mysteries

Usually prayed on Thursdays.

1. The Baptism of Jesus
2. The Wedding at Cana
3. Jesus Announces God's Kingdom and Calls to Conversion
4. The Transfiguration
5. Jesus Gives Us the Holy Eucharist

The Sorrowful Mysteries

Usually prayed on Tuesdays and Fridays.

1. The Agony in the Garden
2. The Scourging at the Pillar
3. The Crowning with Thorns
4. The Carrying of the Cross
5. The Crucifixion

The Glorious Mysteries

Usually prayed on Wednesdays and Sundays.

1. The Resurrection
2. The Ascension
3. The Descent of the Holy Spirit
4. The Assumption
5. The Coronation

HOW TO LOOK UP A PASSAGE IN THE BIBLE

When you see letters and numbers that look like this: **Jn 3:16**, it's a Bible citation, which mean it tells you how to find a certain passage in the Bible. Of course you can always type it in your internet browser and come up with the text of the Bible you need, but here's the way to look it up in an actual Bible.

The first part of the citation refers to the "book" of the Bible. The Bible is really a collection of seventy-three short books printed together in one big volume. Sometimes in a citation the name of the book is written out (John), but often it is abbreviated (Jn). In the front of your Bible, you can find a list of the books and their abbreviations, as well as a table of contents.

The next part, the first number ("3"), refers to the chapter of the book.

The part after the colon ("16") refers to the verse of the chapter. In some Bibles, the verse numbers are printed (very tiny) in the text itself; in other Bibles, the verse numbers run alongside the text, in the margin. (And sometimes the citation has a comma instead of a colon, like this: Jn 3,16.)

So, the citation above is from the Gospel according to John. Go to chapter 3 and find verse 16: "For God so loved the world that he gave his only Son, so that everyone who believes in him may not perish but may have eternal life."

NOTE TO PARENTS AND TEACHERS

The Catholic faith is founded on relationships, beginning with our relationships with God and his Holy Church. It is not surprising that God created a world of interconnected relationships, since God himself exists in a communion of three persons in one God—Father, Son, and Holy Spirit. We call this the Holy Trinity.

In a scientific sense, ecology is the study of relationships between living organisms, including humans, and their physical environment. Ecology can also refer to caring for the environment. For Catholics, ecology is more than science or caring for the environment, although that's certainly part of it.

Catholics practice an *integral ecology*, which recognizes everything as interconnected. Integral ecology connects a wide range of social, moral, religious, and environmental concerns.

Integral ecology recognizes that human beings are a special part of nature, not separate from it. Integral ecology addresses the needs of people, especially people who are poor, marginalized, sick, disabled, outcast, or vulnerable. Integral ecology is pro-life, which means recognizing each human life as precious because every person is made in the image and likeness of God.

People who are poor or vulnerable often suffer the most from a degraded environment, since they often lack access to food, clean water, clean air, shelter, education, jobs, safe neighborhoods, and outdoor spaces.

Wealthy people can also suffer from ***ecological poverty***, often without even knowing it. This is the poverty of living in a biological desert—an ecosystem that has lost its rich biodiversity, order, and beauty. This limits our view of creation and mutes the message of creation given by our Creator.

The concept of environmental stewardship is not new in the Church. From the first pages of the Bible, God calls us to "till and keep" the Earth—to cultivate it and protect it. Many saints, popes, religious, and lay people have spoken about Catholic ecology. This guide celebrates their deep Catholic understanding of faith and ecology.

God provides us with healthy ecosystems because he loves us, and we have a duty to protect these ecosystems. Knowing and living this is integral to our Catholic faith and leads to a healthier and happier future for all of us.

GLOSSARY

abiotic An absence of living organisms; without life.

Act of Contrition A prayer to express sorrow for our sins and to ask for forgiveness.

adaptation The natural process by which an organism becomes fitted to its surroundings or environment.

amphibian An animal that usually spends time both on land and in water.

animals Living creatures that can move but cannot make their own food.

annual A plant that grows from seed once a year.

aquatic Growing, living, or done in water.

arthropods Animals that have a hard outside covering called an exoskeleton. These include insects, crabs, and spiders.

Baptism The first sacrament that welcomes a person into the Catholic Church and cleanses him or her of original sin through water and the word of God and gives the power to become a child of God like Jesus.

being Anything that exists. Sometimes "being" is used to refer only to living things or even only to persons.

biodiversity The variety of living species on Earth, including plants, animals, bacteria, and fungi.

biome A large community of people, plants, animals, and other living things with a similar climate. An area of the planet which can be classified according to the plant and animal life in it.

biosphere The parts of the Earth that support life.

biotic Living, with life.

bird An animal that has wings and feathers and lays eggs.

book of nature A term used by Saint Thérèse of Lisieux to describe how God expresses his word through nature.

botany The study of plants.

canonized The formal declaration, made by the Catholic Church, that a deceased person is in heaven and is therefore a saint. This means that we may honor him or her as a model of faith and an intercessor for us. The person is referred to as a canonized saint.

canopy The highest layer of foliage in a forest. It is made up of the crowns, or tops, of trees.

Canticle of Brother Sun A well-known prayer of Saint Francis of Assisi, written between 1225 and 1226. The praise in the canticle is not addressed to the creatures but to God, their Creator.

carbohydrates Food created by plants.

carnivore An animal that eats other animals for food.

Catechism of the Catholic Church A book, published in 1992, that explains the basic truths of the Catholic faith. Often abbreviated "CCC." It is available online (see Resources, page 177).

Catholic social teaching A guide for our relationships with each other and with all of creation.

chlorophyll Green matter in plant leaves and stems that absorbs energy from sunlight and makes plants able to produce carbohydrates.

climate All weather conditions found in an area over a long period of time.

climate change The result of changes in the Earth's atmosphere (the layer of gas that surrounds Earth), caused by Earth's natural features, people, or other living things. Recent human activities have had a negative impact on the climate.

common good The good of everyone.

common home A term to describe Earth as a home to all the creatures in it.

communion of saints The sharing of God's grace among all members of his Church. This includes people on Earth, souls in purgatory, and the saints in heaven. The word communion means sharing.

community All of the different populations of people and living things (or living creatures) that interact with one another in an area.

coniferous, conifers Plants that have cones, including pine, spruce, fir, cedar, and redwood trees.

consumer An organism that obtains its food by eating other organisms.

covenant A solemn agreement between two persons or groups, which results in a permanent relationship. In the Old Testament, God made and renewed his covenant with Adam and Eve, Noah, Abraham, and Moses. Christ himself, who is God and man, is the New Covenant between God and his people.

creation All that God has created. The making of all material and spiritual beings and things by God. God made all things from nothing. All creation reveals God's love and shows us what God is like.

creature Anything or any person that is created; every being other than the Creator. The sun, moon, stars, world, people, animals, plants, light, darkness, air, and water are all creatures of God. Creatures depend totally on the sustaining power of God

cultivated Raised or grown on a farm, in our yards, or in another controlled condition.

current The flow of a body of water.

deciduous Trees that shed their leaves, mostly in the fall.

decomposer An organism that feeds on dead organic material and adds nutrients to the soil.

desert A very dry biome with thinly scattered plant life. Deserts are the driest biome.

Desert Fathers Early Christian hermits of the third century. They traveled to the desert of Egypt to live solitary lives of prayer. The Desert Fathers are said to be the first examples of monks.

Doctor of the Church A title, given by the Catholic Church, to a well-known teacher whose holy life and writings have been very helpful to the Church. This title has been given to thirty-seven people.

dominion To have dominion means to rule. God gave human beings dominion over creation, so we are to take care of it and use it for the common good.

echolocation The process of locating objects using the echoes of sounds when they bounce off an object.

ecological conversion A change in how we feel, think, and act so that we can better care for our common home. This change of heart and mind in Christ, proposed by Saint John Paul II, includes a sense of gratitude and respect for the whole of God's creation.

ecological poverty The poverty of living in a biological desert—in an ecosystem that has lost its rich biodiversity, order, and beauty. This limits our view of creation and silences the message of creation given by our Creator.

ecology The study of the relationships between living creatures and their environment (all the surrounding living and non-living creatures). The practice of caring for creation.

ecosystem All of the communities of people, plants, animals, and other living and non-living creatures in an area that work together as a whole.

encyclical A special letter written by the pope.

endemic Species found in only one place in the world.

environment All of the physical surroundings on Earth, including everything living and non-living.

ephemeral A perennial plant that springs up quickly and dies back to its underground parts after a short period of growth and reproduction.

epiphytes Plants such as mosses, ferns, algae, and lichens that grow on the surface of other plants, usually trees. Epiphytes have roots that can pull moisture from the air or the surface of the host plant.

erosion A process in which loose earth material, such as soil, rock, and sand, is moved from one place to another.

eternal Having no beginning or end.

fauna Animals associated with an area or time period.

fens Wetlands with high water content during the summer.

flora Plants associated with an area or time period.

foliage The leaves of a plant.

food chain The order in which organisms depend on each other for food. Every ecosystem, or community of living creatures, has one or more food chains.

food web The complex feeding relationships among organisms in a community.

forest An ecosystem filled with trees and underbrush.

freshwater biome A large community of plants and animals that live in freshwater habitats, including streams, rivers, swamps, marshes, ponds, and lakes. Freshwater has a lower salt content than saltwater.

fungus Plant-like organism that lacks chlorophyll and decomposes, or breaks down, its food. (Plural: fungi)

genus A group of species that have similar characteristics. Genus is a category in the biological classification system used by scientists.

grassland A large community of plants and animals that is dominated by grasses.

greenhouse gasses Gasses like carbon dioxide and methane that trap heat from the sun in our air, making our planet hotter.

habitat Place where an organism lives. The habitat provides the types of food, shelter, water, and temperature needed for survival.

herb layer, herbaceous layer The vegetation in the understory of a forest that consists mainly of non-woody plants.

herbivore A consumer that eats plants for food.

Holy Spirit The third Person of the Holy Trinity, who is equal to the Father and the Son. Another name for the Holy Spirit is the Paraclete (which means supporter).

host plant A species of plant that an organism lives and feeds on.

immortal Living forever. Only human beings have immortal souls.

Incarnation The union of the divine and human natures in Jesus. Jesus is the Son of God, so he is divine. He is also the Son of Mary, so he is human. Jesus is one Person with two natures. This is a central Catholic belief.

indicator species A species that indicates the health of an ecosystem by the health of its own population.

Indigenous peoples People who have a special relationship with the land on which they have lived for many generations, sometimes for thousands of years.

intercede To pray for the sake of another person. Mary, angels, saints in heaven, souls in purgatory, and we the faithful on Earth can all make intercession for us and for others.

invasive species A species that moves into an ecosystem as a result of human actions and can reduce or eliminate populations of native species.

invertebrate An animal that does not have a backbone.

Jesus our Lord, our Savior The Son of Mary and the Son of God.

keystone species A species that has so many jobs in an ecosystem that, without them, the entire system would collapse.

larva Immature form of an insect.

Laudato Si' The name of the encyclical letter to the world about the environment written by Pope Francis in 2015. "Laudato si', mi' Signore" means "Praise be to you, my Lord."

lentic Slow or standing—a description of water found in lakes and ponds.

lobe Rounded part of a leaf organ.

lotic Flowing—a description of water found in most streams and rivers.

mammals Animals that provide milk for their young.

marine Having to do with the ocean.

Mary garden A garden of plants named after Mary, usually with a statue of Mary.

metamorphosis The physical changes that some animals go through to become adults.

migrate To move from one place to another at certain times of the year. Migratory describes an animal that migrates.

mysteries of the Rosary Twenty events in the lives of Jesus and Mary. We meditate on these events when we pray the Rosary. See page 179 for a list of these mysteries and directions for praying the Rosary.

native plants Plants that evolved over time in certain places.

natural 1. Something that is found in nature. 2. Something that comes from the nature of a thing.

nature 1. The created universe. 2. The substance or essence of something, from which comes its characteristics and actions.

niche The unique ways in which an organism survives, avoids danger, and obtains food, water, and shelter.

novena A prayer that is said for nine days in a row or once a week for nine weeks.

nurse logs Fallen logs that serve as a place for seedlings to grow.

omnivore An animal that eats both plants and animals.

organism A living creature, also called a living thing.

original sin The first sin, when Adam and Eve did not follow God's will. Also, the effects in us of our first parents' sin.

patron saint A saint to whom a person, group, or place is dedicated. We pray for the saint's intercession and protection.

perennial A plant that lives from year to year.

permafrost A permanent layer of frozen soil.

photosynthesis The process used by green plants to create food from sunlight, water, soil, and air.

pilgrimage A journey to a holy place.

plants A large group of living things that cannot move from place to place. Using energy from sunlight, most plants make their own food from water, nutrients, and air.

pollination The process of how flowers make seeds. Pollination is when the pollen from a plant's flower reaches the flower of another plant of the same species to make seeds. A pollinator is an animal that pollinates plants.

population All the organisms that belong to the same species living in a community.

predator An organism that mainly kills and eats other animals in order to live.

prey An organism that is killed and eaten by predators.

producer An organism, such as a green plant or alga, that uses an outside source of energy like the sun to make its own food.

purgatory The state of purification before entering heaven.

rainforest Thick forest that grows in wet parts of the world.

reforestation The practice of replanting trees in an area where trees have been removed by cutting or fire.

reptiles A category of animals that are covered in thick scales.

riverine Living on or near a river.

Rosary A Catholic prayer during which we reflect on the lives of Jesus and Mary while praying the Our Father and the Hail Mary. Rosary beads are used to keep track of the prayers. There is a guide to praying the Rosary on page 179.

sacrarium A sink or basin that has a drain directly into the Earth. The sacrarium is used to dispose of water that has been used for washing sacred vessels and linens.

Sacred Scripture Another term for the Bible, God's written word to us. The Holy Spirit inspired human authors to write what he wanted to communicate to us. Sacred Scripture and Sacred Tradition are the two ways God's revelation comes to us.

Sacred Tradition The teachings of Christ to the apostles that have been faithfully handed down from one generation to another through the life and worship of the Church. It is through Sacred Tradition that the Holy Spirit makes the risen Jesus present among us, offering us the same Gospel and sacraments he gave to the apostles.

saint A person in heaven who lived a heroically virtuous life, offered his or her life for others, or was martyred for the faith, and who is worthy of imitation. We are all called to be saints.

Saint Kateri Habitat A special habitat that provides food, water, cover, and space for people and wildlife, as well as a place for prayer and contemplation (deep reflective thought), to restore faith and to conserve the material and spiritual ecological gifts of creation. Saint Kateri Habitats help to conserve biodiversity and reduce our impacts on climate change.

saltwater (or marine) biome A large community of plants and animals that live in saltwater habitats, including oceans and bays. Saltwater has a higher salt content than freshwater.

scientific name A two-part name for a species, composed of the general and specific names (genus and species).

shrub layer Layer of woody plants below the forest canopy, comprised of shrubs and saplings (young trees) of those tree species that form the canopy.

sin An act in which a person freely chooses to do what God has forbidden. Sin turns our hearts away from God and others.

snag A standing dead tree. These can often be useful to wildlife.

social Having to do with interactions between living beings. With humans, "social" can mean people talking, working, and playing with each other.

soul The source of life and the immortal spiritual part of us that animates our body.

species A group of living beings that are alike and can create new life with one another.

spiritual world Invisible realities, such as our souls, angels, and God.

subdue To carefully, wisely, and justly use nature in the service of human life. In our relationships with the rest of creation, we should try to act the way God would act.

subspecies A group or subdivision within a species that has become different from other members of the species, but not different enough to be considered a separate species.

sustainable Using materials in a way that will not damage the environment.

temperate deciduous forest A forest that has cold winters and warm summers and is dominated by trees that lose their leaves.

temperate Mild, having neither extremely hot nor extremely cold temperatures.

temperate rainforest A wooded area in a cool, mild climate zone that receives high amounts of rainfall.

tradition Passing something on from one generation to the next.

traditional ecological knowledge (TEK) The knowledge of Indigenous peoples gathered over hundreds or thousands of years through direct contact with nature in the places where they live.

transpiration The process of water moving out of a plant, mainly through its leaves.

Trinity, Holy Trinity The one, true God: three Persons with one divine nature. We call the three Persons the Father, the Son, and the Holy Spirit. This is a central mystery of our faith.

tropical rainforest Dense forest with tall evergreen trees, usually close to the Equator, which receives more than 203 centimeters (80 inches) of rain a year.

tundra A very cold, dry biome with no trees.

understory Ecosystem between the canopy and floor of a forest.

vernal pools Small pools that fill with water after a rain.

vertebrate An animal that has a backbone.

virtue The habit of doing something good that is pleasing to God. The theological virtues of faith, hope, and love are given to us by God. They lead us to believe, trust, and love God.

watershed An area of land where water flows into one common place, like a river, and then to the ocean.

weathering A process in which rock and other material are broken down. Water, wind, chemicals, plants, and animals can cause weathering.

web of life The many ways in which people, plants, and animals are connected.

wisdom A gift of the Holy Spirit that he grants to all who ask for it in faith. Wisdom helps us to see things from God's point of view and to love the things of God, putting God first in everything we do.

Word, The Another name for God the Son, the second Person of the Holy Trinity, who became man.

NOTES

1. Roberto Italo Zanini, *Bakhita: From Slave to Saint* (San Francisco: Ignatius Press, 2013), 36.

2. Thomas Merton, *The Sign of Jonas* (San Diego: Harcourt, 1953), 215–216.

3. Jodyanne Benson, *Behold: A Reflection Journal Where Wonder, Creation, and Stewardship Meet* (self-pub., Thy Olive Tree, 2011), 33.

4. To read more about Catholic Social Teaching, see the website of the United States Conference of Catholic Bishops: https://www.usccb.org/beliefs-and-teachings/what-we-believe/catholic-social-teaching/seven-themes-of-catholic-social-teaching.

5. Pope John Paul II, "General Audience," The Holy See, January 17, 2001, no. 4, https://www.vatican.va/content/john-paul-ii/en/audiences/2001/documents/hf_jp-ii_aud_20010117.html.

6. "Message of His Holiness Pope Benedict XVI for the Celebration of the World Day of Peace," The Holy See, January 1, 2008, no. 7, https://www.vatican.va/content/benedict-xvi/en/messages/peace/documents/hf_ben-xvi_mes_20071208_xli-world-day-peace.html.

7. Pope Francis, *Laudato Si'*, The Holy See, May 24, 2015, https://www.vatican.va/content/francesco/en/encyclicals/documents/papa-francesco_20150524_enciclica-laudato-si.html.

8. *Story of a Soul: The Autobiography of St. Thérèse of Lisieux*, 3rd ed., trans. John Clarke (Washington, D.C.: ICS Publications, 1996), 14.

9. Pope Francis, *Laudato Si'*, no. 230.

10. Hildegard of Bingen, *Scivias*, trans. Columbia Hart and Jane Bishop (Mahwah, NJ: Paulist, 1990), 94.

11. *The First Life of Saint Francis* by Thomas of Celano, in *St. Francis of Assissi: Writings and Early Biographies; English Omnibus of the Sources for the Life of St. Francis*, Marion A. Habig, ed., Raphael Brown et. al, trans. (Chicago: Franciscan Herald, 1983), 278.

12. Francis of Assisi, "The Canticle of the Creatures," in *Francis of Assisi: Early Documents*, Regis J. Armstrong, J. A. Wayne Hellman, William J. Short, eds., vol. 1, *The Saint* (Hyde Park, NY: New City Press, 1999), 113–114, https://franciscantradition.org/francis-of-assisi-early-documents/the-saint/writings-of-francis/the-canticle-of-the-creatures/129-fa-ed-1-page-113. Slightly adapted for this book.

13. Pier Giorgio Frassati to Marco Beltramo, August, 1923, in Maria di Lorenzo, *Blessed Pier Giorgio Frassati: An Ordinary Christian*, trans. Robert Ventresca (Boston: Pauline Books and Media, 2004), 81.

14. Bernard of Clairvaux to Henry Murdoch in Edward Churton, *The Early English Church* (London: James Burns, 1840), 333, https://books.google.com/books?id=6jyNnAf0ml4C&pg=PP11#v=onepage&q&f=false.

15. Thérèse, *Story of a Soul*, 14.

16. Reuben Thwaites, ed., *The Jesuit Relations and Allied Documents* (Cleveland: Burrows Brothers, 1896), quoted in Bruce Henry, *Friends of God: The Early Native Huron Church in Canada*, http://www.wyandot.org/friendsofgod.htm.

17. "Sister Dorothy Stang Novena," Sisters of Notre Dame de Namur, accessed September 11, 2022, p. 2, https://www.sndohio.org/sister-dorothy/dorothy-stang-novena.

18. "Prayer for Healing," Sister Dorothy Stang, Sisters of Notre Dame of Namur, accessed 2022, https://www.notredameonline.org/resources/sister-dorothy-stang/.

19. Annalise Michaelson, email to author, 2022.

20. “Message of His Holiness Pope Francis for the World Day of Prayer for the Care of Creation,” The Holy See, September 1, 2018, https://www.vatican.va/content/francesco/en/messages/pont-messages/2018/documents/papa-francesco_20180901_messaggio-giornata-cura-creato.html.

21. Pope Francis, *Laudato Si’*, no. 246.

ABOUT THE AUTHORS

This book has been written by two Catholic professional ecologists, Kathleen Hoenke and Bill Jacobs. Kat and Bill have more than forty years of combined experience working for major regional and national conservation organizations.

Kathleen "Kat" Hoenke is the Executive Director of the Saint Kateri Conservation Center. Kat is a landscape ecologist and GIS specialist with a Master of Environmental Management Degree in Ecosystem Science and Conservation from Duke University. GIS, or Geographic Information Systems, helps scientists map locations of important habitats, and therefore helps us to prioritize them for restoration and protection. Kat focuses on the ecology of aquatic habitats, and how to restore those habitats to natural, functioning systems for people and wildlife. Kat lives in Maryland with her husband, Kurt, and her two children, Finn and Ella, where they attend St. Margaret Church in Bel Air.

William "Bill" Jacobs is the Founder and Senior Conservation Advisor of the Saint Kateri Conservation Center. Bill is an ecologist and conservationist with a Master of Science Degree in Forest Resources Management from the State University of New York, College of Environmental Science and Forestry (ESF). Bill has worked in conservation for more than thirty years as a consultant and senior ecologist for several governmental and non-governmental organizations, including The Nature Conservancy, GEI Consultants, Long Island Native Plant Initiative (LINPI), and the New York State Department of Environmental Conservation. Bill's work has been featured in the *New York Times*, *National Catholic Register*, *Saint Anthony Messenger*, and EarthBeat. Bill founded the Saint Kateri Conservation Center in 2000. Bill and his wife Lynn have three adult children (Erin, Cara, and Willy) and two grandchildren (Jacob and Jonah). Bill lives in the Diocese of Rockville Centre in New York and attends Saint John the Baptist R.C. Church.

The Saint Kateri Conservation Center is a Catholic non-profit organization that promotes faith, integral ecology, biodiversity, and climate resilience. The Center's programs include Saint Kateri Habitats, Parish Arks, Indigenous Peoples Program, and a Catholic land trust. For more information, visit www.Kateri.org.

ABOUT THE ILLUSTRATOR

Born and bred in Kent, England, **Fiona Osbaldstone** loved painting as a kid and used to paint her versions of the Disney characters. She always wanted to do something with art and went to the Kent Institute of Art and Design to see what the possibilities were. She was inspired by the works of David Shepherd and Norman Rockwell for their detail and diversely different styles. Fiona usually works in watercolour but can also do pencil or acrylics, depending on what is required. Her style is realistic, but not photo realistic; "I just like it to look as it's meant to be." Her work includes natural history, botanical, people, and scenes. Outside of the artistic field, although not too far removed, she loves pottery and makes and sells her own pieces, and she enjoys photography as well as cycling but is "not too good at that and invariably ends up in a ditch."

Who are the Daughters of St. Paul?

We are Catholic sisters with a mission. Our task is to bring the love of Jesus to everyone like Saint Paul did. You can find us in over 50 countries. Our founder, Blessed James Alberione, showed us how to reach out to the world through the media. That's why we publish books, make movies and apps, record music, broadcast on radio, perform concerts, help people at our bookstores, visit parishes, use social media and the Internet, and pray for all of you.